VOICES

WAR, RESISTANCE
FOR FULL-SPEC

EDITED BY T. J. COLES

CLAIRVIEW

Clairview Books Ltd.,
Russet, Sandy Lane,
West Hoathly,
W. Sussex RH19 4QQ

www.clairviewbooks.com

Published in Great Britain in 2017 by Clairview Books

A longer version of this book was published as an ebook by the Plymouth Institute for Peace Research in 2015. This revised edition contains some additional and updated material

© 2017 to T. J. Coles for selection and editorial matter and to the individual authors for their contributions

This book is copyright under the Berne Convention. All rights reserved. Apart from any fair dealing for the purpose of private study, research, criticism or review, no part of this publication may be reproduced, stored in a retrieval system, or transmitted in any form or by any means, electronic, electrical, chemical, mechanical, optical, photocopying, recording or otherwise, without the prior written permission of the copyright owner. Inquiries should be addressed to the Publishers

The rights of the contributors to be identified as authors of this work have been asserted in accordance with sections 77 and 78 of the Copyright, Designs and Patents Act, 1988

A CIP catalogue record for this book is available from the British Library

Print book ISBN 978 1 905570 89 8
Ebook ISBN 978 1 905570 90 4

Cover by Morgan Creative featuring spray can © Fxmdk 73
and OK Bird © Dreamstime.com
Typeset by DP Photosetting, Neath, West Glamorgan
Printed and bound by 4Edge Ltd, Essex

Contents

Introduction: Bad News, Good News   1
T. J. Coles

The Coming War   20
John Pilger

Peace of the Graveyard   24
Noam Chomsky

Reality and the US-made Famine in Yemen   32
Kathy Kelly

Preparing for War with Russia and China: The US Quest for Global Domination Depends on Space Technology   37
Bruce K. Gagnon

A Visit to Russia for 'Life Extension' of the Planet: NATO, Poland and Operation Anakonda   48
Brian Terrell

Where to Turn: War and Peace in Afghanistan and Standing Rock   54
Kathy Kelly

Redefining 'Imminent': How the US Department of Justice Makes Murder Respectable, Kills the Innocent and Jails their Defenders   60
Brian Terrell

America – and why Britain sucks up to it   71
Robin Ramsay

The Enemy is Not Trump, it is Ourselves   81
John Pilger

Historical Perspective of the 2014 Gaza Massacre   90
Ilan Pappé

Terror in Britain: What did the Prime Minister Know?   97
John Pilger

'Je ne sais pas qui je suis': Making Sense of Tragedies like the Charlie Hebdo Incident When the Government Narrative Doesn't Make Sense   104
Cynthia McKinney

About the Contributors   126

Introduction: Bad News, Good News

This book coincides with three commemorations.

The first is the 50th year of Israel's conquest of the remaining Palestinian territories (the West Bank and Gaza) in June 1967, as well as the Syrian Golan Heights and the Egyptian Sinai. (Israel abandoned the Sinai in 1982.) The second is the centenary of the Balfour Declaration: the statement by a British foreign secretary (Arthur Balfour) promising a homeland for both Arabs and Jews. The third is the 70th anniversary of Israel's founding in 1948, at the expense of 700,000 Palestinians who were expelled from their homes. The creation of the State of Israel also created the current refugee crisis for stateless Palestinians, who now number 5 million.[1] *10th anniversary of Gaza blockade*

Israel–Palestine is a symbol of deeper crises in the Middle East. It symbolizes the success of Euro–American propaganda systems in distorting facts and hiding truths from members of the public. A survey conducted by IRmep and Google Consumer Surveys suggests that most Americans (49.2% to 39.8%) think that Palestinians occupy Israel, when the facts are the opposite. More broadly, media distortions and omissions mean that few Westerners realize the extent to which Euro–American bombing has decimated the Middle East and North Africa.[2]

The Israeli occupation of Palestine also symbolizes the region-wide use of proxies for short-term goals. Israel helped the Islamist political group Hamas in the 1980s as a weapon against the secular Palestinian Liberation Organization, which accepted the UN's terms for peace in 1988–89. Hamas became a serious political force after the Israeli settler withdrawal from Gaza in 2005 and the subsequent Israeli military imprisonment of Gaza. Today, few Westerners are aware that many of the terrorists fuelling the fires in the region – particularly the Free Syrian Army and its offshoots – have been organized and trained by the US and its partners, especially the UK. The UN recently reported that Israel was assisting Al-Nusra fighters in Syria, who are battling Israel's enemy, Bashar al-Assad. The trouble is that Al-Nusra (which changed its name to Jabhat Fateh al-Sham) is another name for Al-Qaeda.[3]

The conflict also symbolizes the geostrategic tensions which could very plausibly ignite into nuclear war and end the world.

In 2007, as part of Operation Orchard, Israel attacked an alleged nuclear reactor in Syria. A British minister quoted in *The Spectator* said, 'If people had known how close we came to world war three that day there'd have been mass panic'. Nobody knows what happened, but it is likely that the US raised its nuclear threat level as a warning to Russia not to retaliate against Israeli air strikes against their regional ally, Syria. Israel possesses nuclear weapons, as does its enemy Pakistan, which is also an enemy of the nuclear-armed India. Another official Israeli enemy, Saudi Arabia, has announced plans to develop nuclear weapons in an alleged defence against Iran, which does *not* have nuclear weapons and is not developing them, despite what lying political leaders allied to the US keep claiming.[4]

As millions of Palestinian refugees continue to live in the miserable camps of Jordan, Lebanon and elsewhere, millions

INTRODUCTION: BAD NEWS, GOOD NEWS | 3

more are trapped in the massive US–Israeli-run prison complexes called Gaza and West Bank. They endure periodic massacres like Operations Cast Lead and Protective Edge. The new ultra-right US administration has put paid to any possibility of Israel adhering to international law and the ultra-right Netanyahu government in Israel is committed to further colonization of Palestinian land.[5]

Trump in the White House

Continuing with the threat of nuclear apocalypse:

Businessman Donald Trump wrote about his desire to attack North Korea as early as the year 2000 in his book *The America We Deserve*. Calling North Korea a rogue state, Trump says that although 'China is our biggest long-term challenge ... the biggest [short-term] menace is North Korea'. Trump criticizes Bill Clinton's $4bn aid programme, which allowed North Korea to develop US-supplied fossil fuels and more importantly provided food for the starving population. Offering no evidence, Trump says: 'Just about anywhere America is threatened – by terrorists, by the spread of nuclear weapons and missile technology, you name it – we can count on the folks in Pyongyang to have a hand in it' (pp. 125–132).

During his campaign and after North Korea falsely claimed to have detonated a hydrogen bomb, presidential candidate Trump said that as President he would use China as a proxy to deal with North Korea. Exactly what this would entail, Trump did not say. But as both China and allegedly North Korea have nuclear weapons (as does the US and North Korea's next-door neighbour, Russia), any escalation could be fatal. China, says Trump, holds 'total control over North Korea ... [a]nd China should solve that problem. And if they don't solve the problem, we should make trade very difficult for China'.[6]

By 2007, the US Army's Strategic Studies Institute reckoned that North Korea was looking to unify with South Korea, not remain isolated as international media would have us believe. In 2015, the US Director of National Intelligence stated that one of North Korea's objectives in claiming to possess nuclear weapons and develop warheads is deterrence: to *deter* attacks from the US, South Korea and China. 'We have long assessed that Pyongyang's nuclear capabilities are intended for deterrence, international prestige, and coercive diplomacy'.[7]

Following these events: in its 70th anniversary edition, the *Bulletin of the Atomic Scientists* cautioned that the hands of the Doomsday Clock moved from three- to two-and-a-half-minutes to midnight. The Bulletin was founded by conscientious scientists who had worked on the Manhattan Project, which ultimately brought us nuclear weapons and a giant leap closer to apocalypse. Every year, specialists move the hands back or forth, depending on how close they think we are to terminal danger. Midnight symbolizes the end.

'Over the course of 2016', says the *Bulletin*, 'the global security landscape darkened as the international community failed to come effectively to grips with humanity's most pressing existential threats, nuclear weapons and climate change'. It identifies two main culprits: The United States and Russia. Together, the report continues, these nations 'possess more than 90 percent of the world's nuclear weapons'. Both countries have been facing off 'in a variety of theaters, from Syria to Ukraine to the borders of NATO'. In addition, both

INTRODUCTION: BAD NEWS, GOOD NEWS | 5

are modernizing their nuclear weapons. America is designing small nukes for deployment in war fighting. '[S]erious arms control negotiations were nowhere to be seen.'[8]

Turning to the second main threat to survival, climate change: America's National Aeronautics and Space Administration states: 'Two key climate change indicators – global surface temperatures and Arctic sea ice extent – have broken numerous records through the first half of 2016'. Under Obama, the US agreed to attend a meagre climate conference in Paris (COP21). Citing Reuters, a *Guardian* headline reads: 'Trump seek[s] quickest way to end Paris climate agreement'. In 2016, 65 million people, half of whom children, were – and remain – displaced because of war, flooding, drought, and famine. The UN High Commissioner for Human Rights estimates that every 60 seconds, 24 persons are displaced.[9]

Turning to Western politics:

In its 2016/17 report on the state of the world, Amnesty International notes that '[f]or millions, 2016 was a year of unrelenting misery and fear'. This was symbolized by the election – in the most powerful and influential nation in history – of a man who 'frequently made deeply divisive statements marked by misogyny and xenophobia, and pledged to roll back established civil liberties and introduce policies which would be profoundly inimical to human rights'. The report goes on to say that President Trump's 'poisonous campaign rhetoric exemplifies a global trend towards angrier and more divisive politics'. Yet, the report also notes that the events of 2016 follow a trend. Trump's predecessor, President Obama, 'leaves a legacy that includes many grievous failures to uphold human rights, not least the expansion of the CIA's secretive campaign of drone strikes and the development of a gargantuan mass surveillance machine'.[10]

Meanwhile, Kenneth Roth of Human Rights Watch began his 2017 address warning of the 'cauldron of discontent' facing populations across the world. By appealing to populism, 'certain politicians are flourishing and even gaining power by portraying rights as protecting only the terrorist suspect or the asylum seeker at the expense of the safety, economic welfare, and cultural preferences of the presumed majority'. Roth concludes that this current generation of far-right populists 'scapegoat refugees, immigrant communities, and minorities. Truth is a frequent casualty. Nativism, xenophobia, racism, and Islamophobia are on the rise.'[11]

Oxfam reports that neoliberal economic policies have created a global wealth divide in which just eight individuals own as much wealth as the poorest 3.6 billion. Oxfam notes that, '[f]rom Brexit to the success of Donald Trump's presidential campaign, a worrying rise in racism and the widespread disillusionment with mainstream politics, there are increasing signs that more and more people in rich countries are no longer willing to tolerate the status quo. Why would they', asks Oxfam, 'when experience suggests that what it delivers is wage stagnation, insecure jobs and a widening gap between the haves and the have-nots?' Taking simple steps such as reductions in military spending and taxing the rich would have lifted 700 million people out of poverty over a 20-year period, the report concludes.[12]

The good news is that while rights are in decline, dedicated activists are slowing the acceleration.

INTRODUCTION: BAD NEWS, GOOD NEWS | 7

In 2016, the Afghan Peace Volunteers and Borderfree Street Kids organization visited the Rehabilitation Services for the Blind in Afghanistan (Rayaab). 'They brought MP3 players as gifts to 50 visually impaired students', writes activist Dr Hakim. 'The students will use the MP3 players to listen to recorded school lessons and educational programs.' Rayaab is led by Mahdi Salami and his wife Banafsha, 'who are themselves visually impaired'.[13]

At the local level in Exeter (UK), members of the Palestine Solidarity Campaign (PSC) organized a sponsored walk to raise money for a kindergarten in Umm al-Kheir. The village is in the Palestinian West Bank, which has been occupied illegally by Israel since 1967. 'The villagers are regularly attacked' by Israeli colonizers, says the PSC website. The money raised, £4000, 'will pay for teachers' salaries for a year, equipment and repairs to the kindergarten building. Education is regarded as particularly important by the villagers', the group explains, 'because the settlers and the Israeli army are making it impossible for the villagers to make a living from their traditional employment as herders, so the children will have to train for other work'.[14]

Turning to America, No More Deaths (*No Más Muertes*) is an organization dedicated to ending the deaths and killings of refugees and migrants, including women and children, who attempt to enter the highly-guarded US border with Mexico. As well as fleeing poverty in the latter, many escape gang violence in Guatemala and death squads in Honduras. No More Deaths recently held an art auction in New York to raise money for their aid efforts, which include raising awareness about refugee and migrant rights and providing food and water to exhausted asylum seekers.[15]

Meanwhile in Europe, Refugee Rescue, a team of volunteers, risks lives to save lives. As hundreds of thousands of men, women and children attempt to cross the Mediterranean to escape war, poverty and climate change, the British government – ignoring its obligations under international law – engages in what it calls 'counter-refugee' operations. But Refugee Rescue is having none of it. The organization was 'born in response to the mass displacement of people fleeing war, [including] families who are forced to risk their lives to get to safer lands ... We could not look the other way.'[16]

The above is a tiny, scattered selection from a vast array of individuals and groups working for peace, justice and rights. With very, very few exceptions they are excluded from mainstream media because direct action towards the betterment of society, outside the authorized framework of parliamentary democracy, is extremely dangerous to governing elites. From an elite perspective, it is better to portray the world as relentlessly cruel and people as wholly self-interested, as the media do.

Syria: An Exercise in Denial

One of the most important things we can do is educate ourselves and our colleagues about the nature of war and American imperialism. Russia and China often *respond* to US expansion and aggression, not act aggressively in a political vacuum, as the media would have it. They surely would, had they the power. But the fact is that at this moment in history, America has the power and is seeking to dominate the world accordingly. Today, Syria is at the heart of America's efforts to conquer the Middle East. The West is largely responsible for

INTRODUCTION: BAD NEWS, GOOD NEWS | 9

the carnage in Syria, and because of a media blackout and absence of public figures willing to speak to the facts, very few Westerners know about it.

The BBC's coverage of the US missile attack in early 2017 is a typical example of how Western media operate: how they frame the stories outside any reference to international law; as if the terrorists trying to overthrow Assad are not being trained and organized by the West; how the facts become part of an ideological battle between the inherently moral West and inherently evil East; how it is up to America to lead the world, as if no other countries or the UN matter; and as if civilians are not destroyed by US and British bombs.

In April 2017, chemical weapons were allegedly used to kill civilians in Idlib province. Western media immediately blamed the Russian-backed Assad government, even though Western-backed terrorists possess chemical weapons. Supposedly in response, the Trump administration fired 59 Tomahawk missiles at an air base in Syria, killing seven Syrians, including four children. We only have Russia's figures to go on because the West will not investigate its own war crimes. 'Washington has entered the war against the Assad regime', said BBC Radio 4 presenter John Humphrys. 'It's understood that there were Russians at [the Syrian] airfield.' This means that although America warned Moscow of the impending attack, it was willing to escalate a proxy war with a rival which has nuclear weapons. The Kremlin warned of 'negative consequences' to America's bombing. BBC coverage avoided any mention of nuclear tensions between Russia and the US.[17]

Humphrys interviewed James Jeffrey, the former US Ambassador to Iraq and Deputy National Security Advisor to

George W. Bush. Jeffrey's attitude gives us some insight into the imperial mentality of the US policymaking elite. Jeffrey said that Assad was intent on 'conquering' Syria: that is, intent on conquering his own territory. By implication, *America* owns Syria and by defeating the terrorists, Assad is stealing it from the USA. This imperial mentality is standard among the powerful. In response to America's bombing, Humphrys told Jeffrey to expect a 'profound international reaction', particularly from Russia. Jeffrey replied: 'Who cares?' Who cares if we escalate war to the point of nuclear exchange?[18]

Correspondent Jeremy Bowen said that Trump was trying to gain 'credibility' by bombing Syria, adding, 'in Syria, you get credibility by using force'. Instead of asking what right we have to seek the removal from power of a foreign head of state, Humphrys asked, 'What will it take to bring Assad down?' Bowen said that any Iranian involvement, 'would be a huge escalation'. Notice the inference that America's bombing is not a huge escalation – only enemies like Iran can escalate regional conflicts.[19]

During his interview with UK Defence Secretary Michael Fallon, Humphrys then appeared to endorse illegal war against Assad. 'Isn't there a great degree of moral pressure on countries like the United States, and indeed on us [Britain], to say, actually we want to stop this whole thing now [the war]? We've crossed that red line [by bombing], let's try to finish it. Let's try to put an end to the suffering of the people of Syria.'[20]

Here's the reality about the suffering people of Syria:
America did not 'enter the war' in 2017, as the BBC claims. Britain, America and France *started* the war in 2010. Assad is

INTRODUCTION: BAD NEWS, GOOD NEWS | 11

a brutal dictator – as he was when Britain and America were supporting him before 2011 – and has used extreme violence against legitimate, peaceful demonstrators. But Assad also has a duty to stop Western-backed terrorists from taking over the country. Were it not for the West using these forces as a proxy to depose Assad (as they had in Libya to depose Gaddafi), there would be no war in Syria. Assad would not be using massive amounts of indiscriminate violence across the whole country. The violence Assad used against political opponents could have been constrained via peaceful international pressure on the part of civilians. But peace is not in the interests of political elites: the higher priority is supporting governments who do America's bidding.[21]

Ultimately, Britons, Americans and the French bear most of the responsibility for the 300,000 dead Syrians, the 11 million refugees and the massive infrastructural damage wrought on the country. This assessment is not West-bashing for the sake of it, it is demonstrable:

In 1997, the US committed itself to a doctrine of global militarism called 'Full Spectrum Dominance'. By 2001, the US had invaded Serbia and Afghanistan, and had Iraq under illegal no-fly zone bombardments and illegal, genocidal economic sanctions which various UN representatives say killed a million Iraqis by denying them medicine. After 9/11, former NATO General Wesley Clark saw a Pentagon memo planning to 'take out' seven countries in five years. Syria was one of them. According to various US Congressional and think-tank documents, the aim is to depose various regimes across the Middle East and North Africa (the New Middle East as the Bush administration called it) in order to open US markets. In Syria the aim is this and more: to build pipelines to take energy from the Middle East to the Mediterranean Sea so that the US has control over Middle East oil and trading routes.[22]

France's former Foreign Minister Roland Dumas stated on French television that in 2010, prior to the Syrian Arab Spring, British secret service agents approached him to join them on a foreign rebel 'invasion', in his words, of Syria. It later emerged that Britain had a plan to organize a rebel force of 100,000 terrorists in Syria. This narrative is missing from the BBC, CNN et al. During the Arab Spring, Assad's forces murdered peaceful demonstrators, as did Western allies, including President Saleh of Yemen. The Obama and Cameron regimes unilaterally declared that Assad had lost 'credibility' as a leader and should step down. Britain began working with Islamists in order to form a Transitional National Council, whose armed wing is the Free Syrian Army.[23]

Had he the power, Assad could have invoked the UN Charter, which prohibits the threat of force against a sovereign nation, and launched pre-emptive attacks on the US and Britain. Not that anyone would advocate such a thing, but this is to demonstrate the immorality of using violence in international affairs. It is also important to highlight the law, which is absent from most media discourse.

Paths to Peace

Some simple political solutions to the crises above are as follows: they require dedicated, mass public pressure from populations all over the world in order to force governments to adopt them. This is not to suggest that some earthly paradise will dawn. There will be flare-ups and tensions, but a basic framework for peace will be established.

INTRODUCTION: BAD NEWS, GOOD NEWS | 13

On Israel–Palestine: The Israeli armed forces must withdraw from the territories they occupied in 1967. If Israel wants to build a wall to protect against terrorism, it can do so on its own border, not in Palestinian East Jerusalem. If the illegal Israeli colonizers (tens of thousands of whom are Europeans and Americans who are subsidized by Israel to live in Palestine) want to stay, they can; but not with Israeli military protection. There must be free movement between the Gaza Strip and the West Bank. These core principles are proposed every year at the United Nations General Assembly. Every year, the United States votes no. The reason is that the United States wants to immunize Israel against external constraints because it uses Israel as a military base and regional hi-tech investment hub.[24]

On North Korea: The US has a military base in South Korea and conducts regular joint navy exercises. One way to de-escalate tensions is for the US to withdraw its military base, defer protection of South Korea from potential North Korean aggression (assuming this is a real concern) to the United Nations and to cease all provocative navy exercises. In March 2017, the Trump administration rejected negotiations with North Korea. Another way of easing tensions is to negotiate a deal over its nuclear programme. An even better one is to delegate to the United Nations to broker a deal.[25]

On Syria: The US, Britain, France and Israel must cease all arms flows and training to the anti-Assad terrorists. They must withdraw all forces from the country, especially special operations forces and drones which allegedly target ISIS fighters. Violence only escalates violence. Brokering peace must be deferred to the United Nations. The US and Britain must withdraw their illegal and threatening statements that Assad must stand down before negotiations can begin. By announcing that regime change must be a condition for negotiation, the US and Britain are guaranteeing perpetual war. In October 2016, the US and Britain rejected Russian ceasefire offers. In February 2017, the US-British-backed rebels, who have no legitimacy, rejected peace talks without the precondition of Assad's resignation. Even if the US and Britain cannot be compelled by their internal populations to withdraw from Syria, they can at least be compelled to agree to a ceasefire. They should also put pressure on their rebel proxies to do the same, at the very least.[26]

Let us turn now to the views of activists, academics and journalists on other conflicts, including Iraq and Yemen.

About this Book

In this book, John Pilger contributes two articles. One is about Trump, which exposes the self-serving interests of those 'liberals' who grieve that their pick for the presidency, Hillary Clinton, lost the Electoral College vote. It also examines Obama's shocking human rights record. The second concerns the Manchester 2017 terrorist attacks, which Pilger traces to Britain's internal so-called security service, MI6. In addition, Pilger granted this author an interview in which he discusses the military build-up around China and the subservience his native Australia shows the USA geopolitically.

Noam Chomsky's interview covers everything from Trump to the First World War, global trade, the rise of ISIS, the US-sponsored coup in Ukraine and the US-Israel war on Gaza in 2014.

INTRODUCTION: BAD NEWS, GOOD NEWS | 15

Kathy Kelly — who has been in and out of court and even jail on account of her peaceful, dedicated activism — contributes two articles: the first about Yemen and the human-made famine in the country; the second about war and the path to peace. The second includes information about refugees and the Standing Rock activists.

Bruce Gagnon's article discusses the weaponization of space and the construction of US missile systems around Russia, China and increasingly India in an effort to ensure those countries' integration into the US-led global economy. The Space Command calls this Full Spectrum Dominance.

Brian Terrell contributes two articles: one about drones, activism and the legality of murdering people we don't like and accidentally killing people who happen to be nearby. The other is about US–NATO encroachment on Russia and how military build-ups and exercises raise tensions to dangerous levels.

Robin Ramsay examines the crucial Anglo-American foreign policy relationship, typified by the invasion of Iraq. He argues that British businesses and successive governments hope to piggyback on the economic success of the USA by supporting its brutal foreign policies.

In 2014, Israel slaughtered over 2,000 Palestinians as part of Operation Protective Edge. Ilan Pappé provides some much-needed historical context and shames the international community for its inaction; or, in the case of Europe and the USA, their enabling Israeli war crimes.

Dr Cynthia McKinney provides a vital take on the Truth Movement in her comparative analysis of the famous assassinations of the 1960s (JFK and Dr King) and the more recent Charlie Hebdo attacks. Pieces of the media puzzle just don't fit, argues Dr McKinney. As a result, spontaneous Truth Movements are doing the work of the 'special interest' (or mainstream) media.

T.J. Coles, June 2017

Notes

1. Office of the Historian, 'The 1967 Arab-Israeli War', US Department of State, https://history.state.gov/milestones/1961-1968/arab-israeli-war-1967. Israeli Ministry of Foreign Affairs, 'The Six-Day War (June 1967)', http://www.mfa.gov.il/mfa/aboutisrael/history/pages/the%20six-day%20war%20-%20june%201967.aspx. David S. Robarge, 'CIA analysis of the 1967 Arab-Israeli War', *Getting it Right*, Central Intelligence Agency (US) Library, 15 April 2007, https://www.cia.gov/library/center-for-the-study-of-intelligence/csi-publications/csi-studies/studies/vol49no1/html_files/arab_israeli_war_1.html. United Nations Relief and Works Agency, 'Palestinian refugees', no date (live document), https://www.unrwa.org/palestine-refugees. United Nations High Commission for Refugees and United Nations Relief and Works Agency, 'The United Nations and Palestinian Refugees', January 2007, https://www.unrwa.org/userfiles/2010011791015.pdf.
2. Google Surveys, '1 question from 02/24/16 Occupation US (copy) stat sig', https://surveys.google.com/view?survey=fx4dbfdfoq2ik&question=1&filter=&rw=1.
3. Richard Sale, 'Analysis: Hamas history tied to Israel', United Press International, 18 June 2002, http://www.upi.com/Analysis-Hamas-history-tied-to-Israel/82721024445587/. Israeli Ministry of Foreign Affairs, '408 PLO statement – 7 December 1988', Yearbook, http://mfa.gov.il/MFA/ForeignPolicy/MFADocuments/Yearbook7/Pages/408%20PLO%20Statement-%207%20December%201988.aspx. United Nations Security Council, 'Report of the Secretary-General on the United Nations Disengagement Observer Force for the period from 11 March to 28 May 2014', 10 June 2014, S/2014/401, http://

www.securitycouncilreport.org/atf/cf/%7B65BFCF9B-6D27-4E9C-8CD3-CF6E4FF96FF9%7D/s_2014_401.pdf.

4. James Forsyth and Douglas Davis, 'We came so close to World War Three that day', *The Spectator*, 3 October 2007, https://www.spectator.co.uk/2007/10/we-came-so-close-to-world-war-three-that-day/#.

5. United Nations, 'Report of the Middle East Quartet', 12 February 2016, http://www.un.org/News/dh/infocus/middle_east/Report-of-the-Middle-East-Quartet.pdf.

6. Colin Campbell, 'Donald Trump: Here's how I'd handle that "madman" in North Korea', *Business Insider*, 6 January 2016, www.businessinsider.com/donald-trump-north-korea-china-nuclear-2016-1+&cd=3&hl=en&ct=clnk&gl=uk.

7. Andrew Scobell and John M. Sanford, 'North Korea's military threat: Pyongyang's conventional forces, weapons of mass destruction, and ballistic missiles', Strategic Studies Institute, US Army War College, April 2007, http://www.globalsecurity.org/wmd/library/report/2007/ssi_scobell-sanford.pdf. James R. Clapper, Statement for the Record Worldwide Threat Assessment of the US Intelligence Community Senate Armed Services Committee, 9 February 2016, https://www.armed-services.senate.gov/imo/media/doc/Clapper_02-09-16.pdf.

8. John Mecklin (ed.), 'It is two and a half minutes to midnight: 2017 Doomsday Clock Statement', *Bulletin of the Atomic Scientists*, January 2017, http://thebulletin.org/sites/default/files/Final%202017%20Clock%20Statement.pdf.

9. NASA, '2016 climate trends continue to break records', 19 July 2016, https://www.nasa.gov/feature/goddard/2016/climate-trends-continue-to-break-records. Staff and Agencies, 'Trump seeking quickest way to quit Paris climate agreement, says report', *Guardian*, 13 November 2016, https://www.theguardian.com/us-news/2016/nov/13/trump-looking-at-quickest-way-to-quit-paris-climate-agreement-says-report. UN News Centre, ' "Unprecedented" 65 million people displaced by war and persecution in 2015 – UN', 20 June 2016, http://www.un.org/apps/news/story.asp?NewsID=54269#.WNX7AG81_IU.

10. Amnesty International, *Report 2016/17: The State of the World's Human Rights*, https://www.amnesty.org/en/documents/pol10/4800/2017/en/.
11. Human Rights Watch, *World Report 2017: Events of 2016*, https://www.hrw.org/sites/default/files/world_report_download/wr2017-web.pdf.
12. Oxfam, 'An economy for the 99%', Briefing Paper, January 2017, https://www.oxfam.org/sites/www.oxfam.org/files/file_attachments/bp-economy-for-99-percent-160117-en.pdf.
13. Dr Hakim, 'To touch a colourful Afghanistan', Our Journey to Smile, 22 September 2016, http://ourjourneytosmile.com/blog/2016/09/to-touch-a-colourful-afghanistan/.
14. Exeter Palestine Solidarity Campaign, 'Mailings to our supporters', June 2016, http://www.exeterpsc.org.uk/.
15. No More Deaths, 'No More Deaths Benefit: an art auction to protect the lives of migrants', 22 December 2016, http://forms.nomoredeaths.org/no-more-deaths-benefit-an-art-auction-to-protect-the-lives-of-migrants/.
16. Refugee Rescue, 'About', no date, http://www.refugeerescue.co.uk/about-refugee-rescue/.
17. BBC Radio 4, 'Today', 7 April 2017, http://www.bbc.co.uk/programmes/b08ksck4.
18. Ibid.
19. Ibid.
20. Ibid.
21. For details and sources, see my *Britain's Secret Wars*, 2016, Clairview Books.
22. Ibid. For Clark and the memo, see *Democracy Now!*, 'Gen. Wesley Clark Weighs Presidential Bid: "I Think About It Every Day" ', 2 March 2007, https://www.democracynow.org/2007/3/2/gen_wesley_clark_weighs_presidential_bid.
23. *Britain's Secret Wars*, op. cit.
24. United Nations General Assembly, 'Urging Concerted Action to Revive Peace Talks, General Assembly Adopts Six Resolutions on Question of Palestine, Situation in Middle East', Seventy-first session, 50th meeting,

GA/11861, 30 November 2016, https://www.un.org/press/en/2016/ga11861.doc.htm. International Court of Justice, *Legal Consequences of the Construction of a Wall in the Occupied Palestinian Territory*, 9 July 2004, http://www.icj-cij.org/docket/files/131/1671.pdf. JTA, '15% of settlers are American, new research claims', *Times of Israel*, 28 August 2015, www.timesofisrael.com/15-of-west-bank-settlers-are-americans-new-research-finds/+&cd=5&hl=en&ct=clnk&gl=uk.

25. Mark E. Manyin et al., 'U.S.-South Korea Relations', Congressional Research Service, R41481, 20 October 2016, https://fas.org/sgp/crs/row/R41481.pdf. David E. Sanger, 'Rex Tillerson Rejects Talks With North Korea on Nuclear Program', *New York Times*, 17 March 2017, https://www.nytimes.com/2017/03/17/world/asia/rex-tillerson-north-korea-nuclear.html.

26. Patrick Wintour, 'US and UK reject Russian offer of "pause" in airstrikes on Syria', *Guardian*, 19 October 2016, https://www.theguardian.com/world/2016/oct/18/us-and-uk-reject-russian-offer-of-syria-airstrikes-pause. Patrick Wintour, 'Syria peace talks: rebels appear to rule out ceasefire role for Iran', *Guardian*, 23 January 2017, https://www.theguardian.com/world/2017/jan/23/syria-peace-talks-shaky-start-rebels-refuse-negotiate-face-to-face-astana.

The Coming War

John Pilger

October 2016 and June 2017

[October 2016]

John Pilger: *The Coming War on China* is my 60th film and perhaps one of the most urgent. It continues the theme of illuminating the imposition of great power behind a facade of propaganda as news. In 2011, President Obama announced a 'pivot to Asia' of US forces: almost two-thirds of American naval power would be transferred to Asia and the Pacific by 2020.

The undeclared rationale for this was the 'threat' from China, by some measure now the greatest economic power. The Secretary of Defense, Ash Carter, says US policy is to confront those 'who see America's dominance and want to take that away from us'.

The film examines power in both countries and how nuclear weapons, in American eyes, are the bedrock of its dominance. In its first 'chapter', the film reveals how most of the population of the Marshall Islands in the Pacific were unwittingly made into nuclear guinea pigs in a programme whose secrets – and astonishing archive – are related to the presence of a missile base now targeting China.

T.J. Coles: How do you assess Australia's role in America's 'Pivot to Asia'?

THE COMING WAR | 21

Australia is virtually the 51st state of the US. Although China is Australia's biggest trader, on which much of the national economy relies, 'confronting China' is the diktat from Washington. The Australian political establishment, especially the military and intelligence agencies, are fully integrated into what is known as the 'alliance', along with the dominant Murdoch media. I often feel a certain sadness about the way my own country — with all its resources and opportunities — seems locked into such an unnecessary, dangerous and obsequious role in the world. If the 'pivot' proceeds, Australia could find itself fighting, yet again, a great power's war.

With regards to the British and American media, how can the US get away with selling China as a threat when it is encircling China?

That's a question that goes to the heart of modern-day propaganda. China is encircled by a 'noose' of some 400 US bases, yet the news has ignored this while concentrating on the 'threat' of China building airstrips on disputed islets in the South China Sea, clearly as a defence to a US Navy blockade.

Obama's visit to Japan, and particularly to Hiroshima, was a really cynical act. What is your impression of Japan and the political situation there?

Japan is an American colony in all but name — certainly in terms of its relationship with the rest of the world and especially China. The historian Bruce Cumings explores this in an interview in the film. Within the constraints of American dominance, indeed undeterred by Washington, Japan's current prime minister Shinzo Abe has developed an extreme nationalist position, in which contrition for Japanese actions in the Second World War is anathema and the post-war 'peace constitution' is likely to be changed.

Abe has gone as far as boasting that Japan will use nuclear weapons if it wants. In any US conflict with China, Japan — which last year announced its biggest ever 'defence' budget — would play a critical role. There are 32 US military installations on the Japanese island of Okinawa, facing China. However, there is a sense in modern Asia that power in the world has indeed moved east and peaceful 'Asian solutions' to regional animosities are possible.

What is remarkable about the rise of China is the way it has built, almost in the blink of an eye, a trade, investment and banking structure that rivals that of the Bretton Woods institutions. Unknown to many of us, China is developing its 'New Silk Road' to Europe at an astonishing pace. China's response to threats from Washington is a diplomacy that's tied to this development, and which includes a burgeoning alliance with Russia.

[June 2017]

How do you assess Trump's China policy, as opposed to Obama's?

There isn't a real difference. Obama — urged on by his Secretary of State Hillary Clinton — initiated the so-called

Pivot to Asia, which set the hare running of a US confrontation with China. Trump has seemingly continued this. He has, however, hosted the Chinese president and said what a great guy he is, whatever that's worth.

What is the threat from North Korea?

There isn't a threat from North Korea. The threat is from the United States, which for more than two generations has bullied and provoked North Korea while denying Koreans a treaty that would finally end their civil war and open up numerous possibilities, including reunification. The one pause in this warmongering campaign, during the 1990s, demonstrated that negotiations and the promise of a deal on nuclear power could bring peace to Korea. This was curtailed by George W. Bush.

Do you see much chance of a trade war between the US and China?

No. Their interdependence has never been greater. Trump's election campaign threat to impose 40 per cent tariffs on certain Chinese imports came to nothing. The real threat is a mistaken or accidental missile launch on China — for example, from the US's newly-installed THAAD 'defence system' in South Korea. The unspoken issue is the Pentagon, which has had unprecedented power in Washington since 9/11 and especially since Obama's presidency.

Peace of the Graveyard

Noam Chomsky

October 2014 and March 2017

[October 2014]

T.J. Coles: The years 2014–18 commemorate the centenary of the so-called Great War. What are your reflections?

Noam Chomsky: There is much debate about assignment of responsibility/blame for the outbreak of this horrendous conflict, along with general agreement about one point: There was a high level of accident and contingency; decisions could easily have been different, avoiding catastrophe. There are ominous parallels to nuclear catastrophe.

An investigation of the history of near-confrontations with nuclear weapons reveals how close the world has come to virtual self-annihilation, numerous times, so much so that escape has been a near miracle, one unlikely to be perpetuated for too long. The record underscores the warning of Bertrand Russell and Albert Einstein in 1955 that we face a choice that is 'stark and dreadful and inescapable: Shall we put an end to the human race; or shall mankind renounce war?'

A second no less chilling observation is the alacrity of the rush to war on all sides, in particular the instant dedication of intellectuals to the cause of their own states, with a small fringe of notable exceptions, almost all of whom were punished for their sanity and integrity – a microcosm of the history of the cultivated and educated sectors of society, and the mass hysteria that they often articulate.

What were the real – as opposed to rhetorical – reasons for Israel's assault on Gaza, called Operation Protective Edge?

It is critically important to recognize that a pattern was established almost a decade ago and has been followed regularly since: A ceasefire agreement is reached, Israel makes it clear that it will not observe it and continues its assault on Gaza (and illegal takeover of what it wants elsewhere in the occupied territories), while Hamas observes the ceasefire, as Israel concedes, until some Israeli escalation elicits a Hamas response, offering Israel a pretext for another episode of 'mowing the lawn' (in Israel's elegant parlance).

I have reviewed the record elsewhere; it is unusually clear for historical events. The same pattern holds for Operation Protective Edge. Another of the series of ceasefires had been reached in November 2012. Israel ignored it as usual, Hamas observed it nevertheless. In April 2014, Gaza-based Hamas and the Palestine Authority in the West Bank established a unity government, which at once adopted all of the demands of the Quartet (the US, EU, UN and Russia) and included no Hamas members. Israel was infuriated, and launched a brutal operation in the West Bank, extending to Gaza, targeting mainly Hamas. As always there was a pretext, but it quickly dissolves on inspection. Finally killings in Gaza elicited a Hamas response, followed by Protective Edge.

The reasons for Israel's fury are not obscure. For 20 years, Israel has sought to separate Gaza from the West Bank, with full US support and in strict violation of the Oslo Accords that both had signed, which declare the two to be a single indivisible territorial entity. A look at the map explains the reasons. Gaza offers the only access for Palestine to the outside world; without free access to Gaza, any autonomy that might be granted to some fragmented Palestinian entity in the West Bank will be effectively imprisoned.

What are your thoughts about ISIS and the latest bombing of Iraq?

Reporting is limited, so what we can conclude is necessarily a construction from scattered evidence. To me it looks like this:

ISIS is a real monstrosity, one of the many horrifying consequences of the US sledgehammer, which among other crimes incited sectarian conflicts that may by now have destroyed Iraq finally and are tearing the region to shreds. The almost instantaneous defeat of the Iraqi army was quite an astonishing event. This was an army of 350,000 men, heavily armed, trained by the US for over a decade. The Iraqi army had fought a long and bitter war against Iran through the 1980s. As soon as it was confronted by a few thousand lightly armed militants, the commanding officers fled and the demoralized troops either fled with them or deserted or were massacred.

By now ISIS controls almost all of Anbar province and is not far from Baghdad. With the Iraqi army virtually gone, the fighting in Iraq is in the hands of Shiite militias organized by the sectarian government, which are carrying out crimes against Sunnis that mirror those of ISIS. With crucial assistance from the military wing of the Turkish Kurds, the PKK, the Iraqi Kurdish Peshmerga has apparently held off ISIS. It seems that the PKK are also the most significant force that rescued the Yazidi from extermination and are holding off ISIS in Syria, including the crucial defence of Kobane.

Meanwhile, Turkey has escalated its attacks against the PKK, with US tolerance if not support. It appears that Turkey is satisfied to watch its enemies – ISIS and the Kurds – killing one another within eyesight of the border, with awful consequences likely if the Kurds cannot withstand the ISIS assault on Kobane and beyond.

Another major opponent of ISIS, Iran, is excluded from the US 'coalition' for policy and ideological reasons, as of course is their ally Assad. The US-led coalition includes a few of the Arab oil dictatorships that are themselves supporting competing jihadi groups. The major one, Saudi Arabia, has long been the major source of funding for ISIS as well as providing its ideological roots – no small matter.

ISIS is an extremist offshoot of Saudi Wahabi/Salafi doctrines, themselves an extremist version of Wahabi; and a missionary version, using huge Saudi oil resources to spread their teachings throughout much of the Muslim world. The US, like Britain before it, has tended to support radical fundamentalist Islam in opposition to secular nationalism, and Saudi Arabia has been a primary US ally since the family dictatorship was consolidated and vast oil resources were discovered there.

One of the best informed journalists and analysts of the region right now, Patrick Cockburn, describes US strategy, such as it is, as an Alice-in-Wonderland construction, opposing both ISIS and its main enemies, and loosely incorporating dubious Arab allies with limited European support. An alternative would be to adhere to domestic and international law: appealing to the UN Security Council and then following its lead, and seeking political and diplomatic avenues to escape from the morass or at least mitigate its horrors. But that is almost unthinkable in US political culture.

What are your thoughts about the US–Russia proxy conflict and its potential for nuclear war?

It is an extremely dangerous development, which has been brewing ever since Washington violated its verbal promises to Gorbachev and began expanding NATO to the East, right to Russia's borders, and threatening to incorporate Ukraine, which is of great strategic significance to Russia and of course has close historical and cultural links.

There is a sensible analysis of the situation in the leading establishment journal, *Foreign Affairs*, by international relations specialist John Mearsheimer, entitled 'Why the Ukraine Crisis Is the West's Fault'. The Russian autocracy is far from blameless, but we are now back to earlier comments: we have come perilously close to disaster before, and are toying with catastrophe again. It is not that possible peaceful solutions are lacking.

One final thought, about a dark and menacing cloud that looms over everything we discuss: like the proverbial lemmings, we are marching resolutely towards an environmental crisis that may well displace other concerns in the not too distant future.

[March 2017]

How do you assess the Trump administration's Syria policy?

No strategic policy is discernible. After the chemical warfare atrocity, Trump ordered the bombing of a Syrian airfield that was the alleged source of the attack. It was damaged, but apparently not too severely. Military aircraft were flying bombing missions from there within days. And there was no follow-up. The act seems to have been designed for an American audience, instructed that at last Trump has become a true President. There is little else that suggests some coherent policy or even thought.

Can you talk about Trump's Russia policy?

Trump's actual policies are uncertain, probably even to him. But he has made at least some statements suggesting that he wishes to reduce tensions with Russia, a positive step. The political class is mostly opposed and insisting on more confrontation. The media are keeping to the usual guiding principle: 'objectivity' means reporting accurately what is happening within the circles of political power – 'within the beltway' in the US phrase, similarly in Britain.

And expanding Obama's Pivot to Asia?

The general context is Trump's commitment to militarism and private wealth and power, with the burden falling on the working class and the poor and vulnerable. He is intent on 'rebuilding our depleted military', already by far the most advanced and powerful in world history, far ahead of any conceivable group of competitors, and providing more authority to the military to act free from civilian control. 'America first', with a big fist but no nonsense about diplomacy and 'soft power'.

How do you see the future of global trade under Trump?

Trump claims to be opposed to the [Trans-Pacific Partnership and Transatlantic Trade and Investment Partnership] deals, but has given no indication of what he prefers in their place. He has given no clear ideas about what he thinks of the EU, just random arrows in all directions. One of his few fairly clear positions is support for the most extreme-right sectors in Israel, though even here he has hedged slightly. The rest remains obscure.

The political leaders in South America are moving more to the right. How do you see the future of the region?

The left/centre-left governments of recent years achieved meaningful progress: sharp reduction in poverty, improvements in social justice, freeing the region from the clutches of the IMF (a.k.a. US Treasury Department), and others. They also made many mistakes, crucially reliance on primary product export instead of diversifying the economy, and joining in the elite practice of massive corruption. Many of the successes will probably survive the current regression, quite severe particularly in Brazil, the most important country of the region. I suspect that this too will pass, and there will be a return to a more promising course of social and economic development.

What are the prospects for peace in Palestine under Trump?

Even lower than they have been for some time — unless we mean 'the peace of the graveyard'.

Reality and the US-made Famine in Yemen

Kathy Kelly

March 2017

This week at the Voices for Creative Nonviolence office in Chicago, my colleague Sabia Rigby prepared a presentation for a local high school. She'll team up with a young friend of ours, himself a refugee from Iraq, to talk about refugee crises driven by war. Sabia recently returned from Kabul where she helped document the young Afghan Peace Volunteers' efforts to help bring warmth, food and education to internally displaced families living in makeshift camps, having fled the Afghan War when it raged near their former homes.

Last year Sabia had been visiting with refugees in 'the Calais Jungle', who were fleeing the Middle East and several African countries for Britain. Thwarted from crossing the English Channel, a large mass of people were stopped in this refugee camp in Calais, France, from which French authorities eventually evacuated them, defying their careful solidarity and burning their camp to the ground. As part of her high school talk, Sabia prepared a handout to show where refugees are the most welcomed. One detail astonished her.

In 2016, the US admitted 84,995 refugees, but Yemen, the poorest country in the Arab world, took in 117,000 new refugees and migrants in 2016, and hosts more than 255,000 refugees from Somalia. Yemen is now beginning to host the world's worst humanitarian crisis. What's more, the country is regularly targeted by Saudi and US air strikes.

Since we are also planning a week of fast action related to the tragic circumstances Yemen faces, we were astounded when we realized Yemen is a path of escape for Somalis fleeing the Horn of Africa, refugees of one conflict, stranded in their flight, and trapped in a country where deadly conflict is precipitating into deadlier famine.

After years of US support for dictator Ali Abdullah Saleh, civil war has wracked Yemen since 2014. Its neighbour Saudi Arabia, itself among the region's cruellest dictatorships and a staunch US ally, became nervous in 2015 about the outcome and, with support from nine regional allies, began subjecting the country to a punishing barrage of air strikes, and also imposed a blockade that ended the inflow of food and supplies to Yemen through a major port. This was accomplished with massive, ongoing weapons shipments from the US, which has also waged independent air strikes that have killed dozens of civilians, including women and children.

Pummelled by air strikes and fighting, facing economic collapse and on the brink of famine, how could this tiny, impoverished country absorb thousands upon thousands of desperate migrants? Yemen imports 90% of its food. Because of the blockade, food and fuel prices are rising and scarcity is at crisis levels.

UNICEF estimates that more than 460,000 children in Yemen face severe malnutrition, and 3.3 million children and pregnant or lactating women suffer acute malnutrition. More than 10,000 people have been killed, including 1,564 children, and millions have been displaced from their homes, but worse is the groundwork laid for the far greater devastation of famine. Iona Craig, in the IRIN publication, recently wrote:

> In the middle of a vast expanse of grey scrubland, a rapidly growing population of more than 120 families huddle under parched trees. Escaping the latest wave of conflict on Yemen's Red Sea coast, they walked two days to get to this camp southwest of Taiz city.

But on arrival, the scores of women and children found nothing. No support from aid agencies. No food. No water. No shelter. The elderly talk of eating the trees to survive, while children beg for water from local farmers. A mother cradles her clearly malnourished baby in her arms. Now comes word that on 16 March, 42 Somali people were killed in sustained gunfire from the air as they set forth in a boat attempting to flee Yemen.

'I took cover in the belly of the ship', said Ibrahim Ali Zeyad, a Somali who survived the attack. 'People were falling left and right. Everyone kept screaming, "We are Somali! We are Somali!" But the shooting continued for what felt like half an hour.'

The attack on Yemen traps both Yemenis and fleeing Somalis in the worst of four developing crises which collectively amount, one UN official warns, to the worst humanitarian crisis in the history of the UN. As of this writing, no one has taken responsibility for the strike, but survivors say they were attacked by a helicopter gunship. The boat was carrying 140 people as it headed north off the coast of Yemen.

Meanwhile, US weapons makers, including General Dynamics, Raytheon and Lockheed Martin, profit massively from weapon sales to Saudi Arabia. In December, 2016,

Medea Benjamin wrote: 'Despite the repressive nature of the Saudi regime, U.S. governments have not only supported the Saudis on the diplomatic front, but militarily. Under the Obama administration, this has translated into massive weapons sales of $115 billion.'

At this critical juncture, all member states of the UN must call for an end to the blockade and air strikes, a silencing of all guns, and a negotiated settlement to the war in Yemen. The worst malefactors, the US and Saudi Arabia, must abandon cynical manoeuvring against rivals like Iran, in the face of such an unspeakable human cost as Yemen is being made to pay. US people bear responsibility to demand a radical departure from US policy, which exacerbates the deadly tragedy faced by people living in Yemen.

Choosing a path of clear opposition to US policies towards Yemen, US citizens should demand elected representatives stop all drone attacks and military 'special operations' within Yemen, end all US weapon sales and military aid to Saudi Arabia, and provide compensation to those who suffered losses caused by US attacks.

Our group of activists long functioned under the name 'Voices in the Wilderness', a campaign to defy US economic warfare against Iraq, a form of war through imposition of economic sanctions which directly contributed to the deaths of over 500,000 children. Lost in a culture of hostile unreality and unbearable silence concerning economic warfare, we were evoking, perhaps unconsciously, the plight of refugees seeking survival. We didn't succeed in lifting the brutal economic sanctions against Iraq, but we surely learned harsh realities about how callous and reckless US policy makers could be.

We must ground ourselves in reality and in solidarity with the greater part of the world's people. As our neighbours around the world flee in desperation across borders or within the confines of their own countries, we must continually educate ourselves about the reality of what our nation's actions mean to the world's poor. Building towards a time when our voices may unite and be heard, we must raise them now in crying out for the people of Yemen.

Preparing for War with Russia and China: The US Quest for Global Domination Depends on Space Technology

Bruce K. Gagnon

October 2016

The US, dragging the western allies behind them, is preparing for war with Russia and China. Washington also wants India 'onside' for obvious reasons of geography, history, and growing economic power. The US also needs allies with some money to help pay for the Pentagon's endless war machine that is heavily dependent on expensive space technology.

Getting India 'Onside'

Washington wishes to bring India under its 'Space Command' so that all its military will be run through the Pentagon space warfighting satellite programme. A term 'interoperability' has been coined to describe the process where all allies must have suitable warfighting systems that can be technically run through the US Space Command system. In the end this means the US is controlling the deadly tip of the spear because no other nation has all the satellites and ground stations around the globe that give Washington the ability to see everything on Earth, hear everything, and ultimately target every place on the planet.

All the new NATO allies (and 'partners' like Japan, South Korea, Australia, New Zealand) are being brought into the global military alliance to control and dominate the planet on behalf of western corporate capitalism. That means London–Washington–Brussels–Paris–Berlin running the world. Russia, China, Iran, Syria, North Korea, Brazil, Venezuela, Cuba and a few other nations are on the list for 'regime change' in the coming years. They still stand outside full control by the western bankers and militarists.

The recent formation of the BRICS (Brazil, Russia, India, China and South Africa) alternative economic institution would loan money to developing countries and not exploit them the way western bankers do using the IMF and World Bank as their tools of domination. The West is not happy about BRICS and thus we saw the leader of Brazil was recently dethroned in a coup essentially orchestrated by Washington.

The US–NATO alliance is not happy to currently see many nations around the world begin to stand up against this long run of Western imperialism. The BRICS nations are calling for a multi-polar world and the US demands to remain as the unipolar leader of the planet. Washington appears willing to go to war to defend its collapsing empire.

The US is like a cowboy gambler with a black hat on a Mississippi riverboat playing cards. The cowboy looks around and sees himself surrounded by those he has exploited for years. He thinks his only way out is to start shooting – the law of the west. That, I think, is essentially still the foreign and military policy of the US. It's part arrogance and part fear that the world has woken up at last and is rejecting the cowboy mentality of 'full spectrum dominance'.

A History of Dominance
Growing global poverty and the reality of climate change

though are banging on Washington's front door. The corporations are trying to make money from climate change – their love for the dollar bill is so great that they cannot see beyond their lust for power and greed. I call them pirates.

The pirates have buried a treasure chest in the US – it is our national treasury created from the taxes from the people's hard work. About 55% of every federal tax dollar under the discretion of Congress goes to the Pentagon. America has become a war culture. Our economy is addicted to military production. People are increasingly being indoctrinated that the 'Muslims' are coming to attack us so we must spend more on weapons for war and we must have the very best space technology system in place to protect ourselves. We are a paranoid nation – massive guilt and fear comes from our long legacy of genocide.

First was the destruction of the Native Americans and then the illegal and immoral importation of slaves from Africa. During the days of slavery that very institution became America's dominant economic institution. Slave labour made America rich. This (let's call it fascist) element of our culture might have lost the civil war in the 1860s but they are running the country today. We have a wedding in America of the government and corporate power – they are one in the same. Democracy has been drowned in the United States.

Thus no one anywhere on our Mother Earth should ever listen to the moralistic preaching that comes from Washington about democracy, freedom, peace, or the rule of law. It's all Hollywood talk – a scripted propaganda machine that has sold an image to the world. Fortunately the initial shine has worn off the Stars & Stripes and most people around the globe clearly understand what is really going on.

The 'Pivot to Asia'

I have been working on space issues for the last 33 years and today coordinate the Global Network Against Weapons & Nuclear Power in Space. We are very worried about aggressive US moves to create more conflict with Russia and China – in particular the Pentagon claim that the US Space Command should 'control and dominate space and deny other nations the use of space'.

The dangerous notion of US 'exceptionalism' has now been extended to outer space. In order to successfully operate, the current US global space warfighting system 'downlink ground stations' have been based around the world to relay military communications from one place to another via space satellites. Activists around the planet are opposing the presence of these Star Wars bases in their communities and are the active membership of the Global Network.

The US today is feverishly deploying so-called 'Missile Defense' (MD) systems around the globe – essentially encircling Russia and China. Added to that is Obama's provocative 'pivot' of 60% of US military forces into the Asia–Pacific – what the Pentagon calls 'rebalancing'. This pivot is dangerous and hugely expensive, so costly that Washington's allies are being pressured to help pay for the programme.

China imports 80% of its resources on ships and thus we see the Pentagon 'pivot' as a military strategy to possibly block China's sea routes – literally putting a loaded gun to Beijing's head. China has responded by building a couple of new bases on tiny coral reefs to ensure their unhampered access to the sea lanes in their region.

Last summer the Global Network held its 23rd annual

space conference in Kyoto, Japan. We were invited to meet in Kyoto in order to show support for the campaign opposing the recently deployed US MD radar at Kyogamisaki in the Kyoto prefecture. One day during the conference we took a bus ride to have lunch with the Ukawa villagers and then joined them in a protest at the base.

The MD radar base at Kyogamisaki would assist the Pentagon's attempt to intercept Chinese retaliatory nuclear missiles that they would fire after the US launched a first-strike attack. We are constantly told that MD is being deployed by the Pentagon in Japan, Okinawa, South Korea, Taiwan, Guam, the Philippines and Australia to protect against North Korean missiles. This is a lie and a tactic to redirect the discussion. In fact the US is deploying MD to be able to control and dominate China and Russia.

I'll never forget a few years ago, when North Korea test fired a rocket, I read a story in a space industry publication that quoted US military personnel who were laughing at North Korea. One US airman said that North Korea had virtually no space technology and thus could not really track their own rocket while the US, with its robust space capability, could follow the North Korean rocket with no trouble at all. This made it clear to me that the Pentagon over-hypes the threat from Pyongyang. The truth is that the US is aiming their massive space-directed military machine at Beijing and Moscow.

Missile Offence

MD used to be illegal under the Anti-Ballistic Missile (ABM) Treaty between Russia and the US. Both sides knew that MD is a destabilizing programme that would give one side an advantage over the other. MD's key job is to be the shield that is used to pick-off a nation's nuclear retaliatory capability after the Pentagon's first-strike sword lunges into the heart of the opponent's nuclear forces.

One of the very first things President George W. Bush did after taking office in 2001 was to give Russia notice that the US was pulling out of the ABM Treaty. Since that time, US research, development, testing and deployment of MD systems has been on steroids. At the time of the collapse of the former Soviet Union the US promised that NATO would not expand one centimetre towards Russia. Since then that promise has been repeatedly broken and today NATO has established bases along Russia's border in Latvia, Lithuania and Estonia. Pentagon MD systems were this year deployed in Romania and next year will be deployed in Poland. US Navy Aegis destroyers also carry MD interceptor missiles on-board and today are being deployed in the waters off the coasts of Russia and China.

In early 2014 the US spent $5 billion in a coup d'état in Ukraine that took down an elected government and replaced it with a government in the capital city of Kiev that included Nazis. The US has established a base in western Ukraine where Army Special Forces troops come from the US to train neo-Nazis that have been assigned to the newly created Ukrainian National Guard. These forces have then gone to eastern Ukraine, along the Russian border, where for the last two years they have killed thousands of innocent citizens by shelling their homes, hospitals, churches, schools, day care centres, airports and rail stations. The only crime of the people in eastern Ukraine is that they are of Russian ethnic origin.

PREPARING FOR WAR WITH RUSSIA AND CHINA | 43

The US intends to destabilize Ukraine in order to ultimately force regime change in Moscow. One reason for this is that, because of climate change, the Arctic Sea ice is melting and the oil corporations are eager to drill in the once frozen Arctic region. But Russia has the largest land border, thus the supposed need to break the large Russian Federation into pieces (like happened to Yugoslavia during the presidency of Bill Clinton). By doing this the oil companies believe they'd have an easier time in grabbing the oil near the Russian Arctic coastline.

The Pentagon is deploying four basic MD systems today. Inside the US (California and Alaska) are Ground-Based Midcourse MD interceptors buried deep underground. Their job is to hit a bullet with a bullet in deep space after a retaliatory strike by Russia or China. This programme has the most difficult technical task and has the worst testing results.

In order to increase the chances of being able to knock missiles out of the sky it helps to put the MD interceptors closer to the intended targets. Thus the US is deploying MD systems on Navy Aegis destroyers and porting them in Japan, South Korea, the Philippines and Guam. These ship-based interceptors have the best testing success rates.

Mobile ground-based MD interceptors like the Patriot (PAC-3) and Theater High Altitude Area Defense (THAAD) are used to knock out incoming missiles in the terminal phase. These systems are now being deployed in Japan, Okinawa, South Korea and Guam.

Missiles in Asia

This past August I spent three weeks in South Korea attending various protests against the announced deployment of the

US THAAD 'missile defense' system. The Pentagon plans to station THAAD in the farming village of Seongju (population 10,000). The right-wing South Korean government, following orders from Washington, likely chose this village because it had backed the conservative government by a margin of 85 per cent in the last national election. But that has now changed.

Just before I arrived in South Korea the residents of Seongju held a mock funeral where they announced that they had, en masse, resigned from the ruling party. Then, just before I left Korea, 900 of these same residents took the sacred step of sitting together and shaving their heads. In Korea this is a big deal. It indicates the commitment to fight to the death, and in this case many women also joined the hair shaving, which is rare. This anti-THAAD movement has become a national issue and one of the top concerns for the peace movement in South Korea today. So the US is currently developing MD systems to hit nuclear missiles in the boost phase, mid-course phase and the terminal phase. This clearly indicates the seriousness that the Pentagon attaches to being able to launch a first-strike attack on China and/or Russia and then knock out any retaliatory strike they might be able to fire in return.

MD is not just a theoretical programme. The US Space Command holds a computer war game each year where they practise such a first-strike attack – they call it the 'Blue' team against the 'Red' team. In the war game a US first-strike is launched against Russia and China. When they respond by firing their own nuclear missiles that have survived the initial Pentagon attack, the Space Command's MD systems go to work to pick-off the remaining missiles.

Of course, in the real world things don't always work out so nicely. But the main point is that the Pentagon is actively preparing for such a first-strike attack. The Pentagon deployments of MD interceptor missiles and radars gives Space Command the confidence (and arrogance) that they can use this system. Thus MD becomes highly destabilizing and very dangerous to world peace. While in Okinawa in late 2015 on a solidarity trip to stand with those actively opposing US expanding bases on their island, I spotted a base called Fort Buckner which plays a critical role in 'inter-base, tactical and strategic Command, Control, Communications and Computer (C4) network support of joint Pacific war fighters'. Fort Buckner relays military satellite communications between bases in South Korea, Japan, Okinawa, Guam, the Philippines, Hawaii and the Pentagon.

Triggering WWIII

Sadly Washington is now run by corporate interests who have determined that America's role under globalization of the world economy will be 'security export', which translates to endless war. The number one industrial export product of the US today is weapons. When weapons are your #1 industrial export, what is the global marketing strategy for that product line?

Despite Pentagon claims that they are out to create peace, democracy and stability around the world with their more than 800 military bases, quite the opposite is the truth. I came away from recent trips to Japan, Okinawa and South Korea seeing that the expansion of US bases in the Asia-Pacific is largely about creating the military infrastructure to take down China and Russia.

Add up the current US 'pivot' into the Asia-Pacific; the Japanese Shinzo Abe government's 'reinterpretation' of peaceful Article 9 in their constitution to allow Tokyo to deploy offensive military forces; the destabilizing US-Japan-South Korean military alliance; and we find the makings of a very aggressive programme that could easily trigger World War III.

The Chinese and Russian governments have repeatedly said that they would like to reduce their nuclear forces but cannot do it as long as the US is encircling their countries with MD systems. China and Russia each year go to the United Nations and introduce a new treaty to ban all weapons in space. The US and Israel (which has 200 nuclear weapons) annually block serious negotiations on that important treaty. Both Russia and China have been forced to expand their military operations and to even build more nuclear weapons as they face the US MD programme and an expanding NATO.

When Japan recently launched a satellite into space few took notice. When North Korea launches a satellite or test fires a missile, the world screams bloody murder. Clearly the US and its allies are hypocrites as they lecture North Korea and Iran about weapons of mass destruction but at the same time they are creating the largest military build-up in world history. US foreign military occupation must end if there will ever be true world peace. The Global Network is determined to do what we can to help build such a peace with justice. We are grateful to those in India who are working so hard to put an end to this madness.

We need peace workers in India to educate your fellow citizens about US plans to bring Delhi into the Pentagon's Space Command programme aimed at China. We hope you can help prevent this growing danger of WWIII that could consume the entire planet in a hell fire of nuclear war. Our governments need to be dealing with the reality of climate change and growing global poverty. We must demand they convert the expensive military industrial complex to sustainable technology development to help us protect the future generations. Keep going – we all need each other. Holding hands, let us work together.

A Visit to Russia for 'Life Extension' of the Planet: NATO, Poland and Operation Anakonda

Brian Terrell

November 2016

On 9 October, I was in the Nevada desert with Catholic Workers from around the world for an action of prayer and non-violent resistance at what is now called the Nevada National Security Site, the test site where between 1951 and 1992, 928 documented atmospheric and underground nuclear tests occurred. Since the Comprehensive Nuclear-Test Ban Treaty and the apparent end of the Cold War, the National Nuclear Security Administration, NNSA, has maintained the site, circumventing the intent of the treaty with a stated 'mission to maintain the stockpile without explosive underground nuclear testing'.

Three days earlier, as if to remind us that the test site is not a relic with exclusively historic significance, the NNSA announced that earlier in the month, two B-2 Stealth Bombers from Whiteman Air Force Base in Missouri dropped two dummy B61 nuclear bombs at the site. 'The primary objective of flight testing is to obtain reliability, accuracy, and performance data under operationally representative conditions', said the NNSA press release. 'Such testing is part of the qualification process of current alterations and life extension programs for weapon systems.'

'The B61 is a critical element of the U.S. nuclear triad and the extended deterrent', said Brig. Gen. Michael Lutton, NNSA's principal assistant deputy administrator for military application. 'The recent surveillance flight tests demonstrate NNSA's commitment to ensure all weapon systems are safe, secure, and effective.'

General Lutton and the NNSA do not explain what threat the testing of B61 nuclear bombs is meant to deter. The military industrial complex, including the 'life extension programs for weapon systems' that the US intends to spend a trillion dollars on over the next decades, is not a response to any real threat but exists only to perpetuate itself. For public consumption, however, expenditures of this magnitude require justification. The not so subtle message that this was a 'dry run' of a nuclear attack on Russia was not missed by the media that picked up the story.

Shortly after leaving Nevada, I was in Moscow, Russia, as part of a small delegation representing Voices for Creative Nonviolence from the United States and United Kingdom. Over the next ten days in Moscow and St Petersburg, we saw nothing of the massive preparations for war there that are being reported in the Western media. We saw no sign of and no one we spoke to knew anything about the widely reported evacuation of 40 million Russians in a civil defence drill. 'Is Putin preparing for WW3?', asked one UK tabloid on 14 October: 'Following a breakdown in communication between the USA and Russia, the Kremlin organized the huge emergency practice drill – either as a show of force or something more sinister.' This drill turned out to be an annual review that firefighters, hospital workers and police routinely conduct to evaluate their capacities to manage potential natural and manmade disasters.

Over the past years I have visited many of the world's major cities and Moscow and St Petersburg are the least militarized of any I've seen. Visiting the White House in Washington, D.C., for example, one cannot miss seeing uniformed Secret Service agents with automatic weapons patrolling the fence line and the silhouettes of snipers on the roof. In contrast, even at Red Square and the Kremlin, the seat of the Russian government, only a few lightly armed police officers are visible. They seemed mainly occupied with giving directions to tourists.

Travelling on the cheap, lodging in hostels, eating in cafeterias and taking public transportation is a great way to visit any region and it gave us opportunities to meet people we would not otherwise have met. We followed up on contacts made by friends who had visited Russia earlier and we found ourselves in a number of Russian homes. We did take in some of the sights, museums, cathedrals, a boat ride on the Neva, etc., but we also visited a homeless shelter and offices of human rights groups and attended a Quaker meeting. On one occasion we were invited to address students in a language school in a formal setting, but most of our encounters were small and personal and we did more listening than talking.

I am not sure that the term 'Citizen Diplomacy' can be accurately applied to what we did and experienced in Russia. Certainly the four of us, me from Iowa, Erica Brock from New York, David Smith-Ferri from California and Susan Clarkson from England, hoped that by meeting Russian citizens we could help foster better relations between our nations. On the other hand, as much as the term suggests that we were acting even informally to defend or explain our governments' actions, interests and policies, we were not diplomats. We did not go to Russia with the intention of putting a human face on or in any way justifying our countries' policies toward Russia. There is a sense, though, that the only genuine diplomatic efforts being made between the US and NATO countries at this time are citizen initiatives like our own little delegation. What the US State Department calls 'diplomacy' is actually aggression by another name and it is questionable whether the US is capable of true diplomacy while it surrounds Russia with military bases and 'missile defense' systems and carries out massive military manoeuvres near its borders.

I am conscious of the need to be humble and not to overstate or claim any expertise. Our visit was less than two weeks long and we saw little of a vast country. Our hosts reminded us continually that the lifestyles and views of Russians outside their country's largest cities might be different from theirs. Still, there is so little knowledge of what is going on in Russia today that we need to speak the little we have to offer.

While we heard a wide variety of views on many crucial issues, there seems to be a consensus among those we met about the impossibility of a war between Russia and US/NATO. The war that many of our politicians and pundits see clearly on the horizon as inevitable is not only unlikely, it is unthinkable to the Russian people we talked with. None of them thinks that our countries' leaders would be so crazy as to allow the tensions between them to bring us to a nuclear war.

In the United States, Presidents Bush and Obama are often credited for 'fighting the war over there so we don't have to fight it here'. In St Petersburg we visited the Piskaya Memorial Park, where hundreds of thousands of the one million victims of Germany's siege of Leningrad are buried in mass graves. In World War II, more than 22 million Russians were killed, most of these civilians. Russians, more than Americans, know that the next world war will not be fought on a faraway battlefield.

Russian students laughed at the joke, 'If the Russians are not trying to provoke a war, why did they put their country in the middle of all these U.S. military bases?' But I ruefully told them that due to our nation's professed exceptionalism, many Americans would not see the humour in it. Rather, a double standard is considered normal. When Russia responds to military manoeuvres by the US and its NATO allies on its borders by increasing its defence readiness inside its borders, this is perceived as a dangerous sign of aggression. This summer in Poland, for example, thousands of US troops participated in NATO military manoeuvres, 'Operation Anakonda' (even spelled with a 'k', an anaconda is a snake that kills its victim by surrounding and squeezing it to death) and when Russia responded by augmenting its own troops inside Russia, this response was regarded a threat. The hyped-up proposition that Russia might be conducting civil defence drills raises suspicion that Russia is preparing to launch World War III. Yet a practice run, dropping mock nuclear bombs in Nevada, is not viewed in the West 'as a show of force or something more sinister', but only as an indication of a 'commitment to ensure all weapon systems are safe, secure, and effective'.

The life extension of our planet needs to be a universal goal. To speak of, let alone pour a nation's wealth into a programme of 'life extension programs for weapon systems' is nothing short of madness. Our Russian friends' confidence in our collective sanity and the steadiness of our leadership, especially in the wake of the recent election, is a great challenge. I am grateful to new friends for the warmth and generosity of their welcome and I hope to visit Russia again before long. As important and satisfying as these 'citizen diplomatic' encounters are, however, we must honour these friendships through active resistance to the arrogance and exceptionalism that might lead the US to a war that could destroy us all.

Where to Turn: War and Peace in Afghanistan and Standing Rock

Kathy Kelly

November 2016

In July 1941, Albert Einstein, ten months a US citizen, wrote Eleanor Roosevelt asking her, as First Lady, to raise with the president the matter of lifting bureaucratic hurdles so that Jewish refugees, threatened by Hitler's Final Solution, could be granted entry into the US. 'I know of no one else to whom to turn for help', he wrote. But the US government chose not to heed Einstein's appeal. The following year, some 2.7 million Jews — nearly half of all Jewish victims of the Holocaust — were annihilated.

Throughout 2016, as millions overseas faced First World refugee policies, with consequences ranging from the cruel to the brutal to the lethal, it has seemed increasingly unlikely that any US voice — save, perhaps, US citizens' voices raised in unlikely unison — could sway the US White House to give comfort to those fleeing the chaos and death that US wars have sown in Iraq and Afghanistan.

'We need to have people who mean something to us', Bernard Cooke once wrote. 'People to whom we can turn knowing that being with them is coming home.' His words make me think of Zekerullah, a coordinator of the Afghan Peace Volunteers' 'Street Kids School'. He recently stood in front of the dried up, stench ridden, polluted Kabul River, filming a video encouraging Standing Rock indigenous activists never to give up, even in the face of armed police, and never to let what happened to the Kabul River befall their beautiful Missouri. Kabul is the safest place in Afghanistan, a 'Ka-bubble' governed in partial, fragile security by the US allied local government. The Afghan Peace Volunteers, mainly based in Kabul, are no strangers to fear, penury, loss and the dangers of living in a war zone, in a poisonous atmosphere. Yet instead of exacerbating divisions, they have befriended child labourers, street vendors and trash collectors, by creating a school which now serves one hundred children. This enables them to catch up with the state schools' math and language curriculum while compensating their families with monthly donations of rice and oil.

A 2016 Human Rights Watch report notes:

At least a quarter of Afghan children between ages 5 and 14 work for a living to help their families. Many are employed in jobs that can result in illness, injury, or even death due to hazardous working conditions and poor enforcement of safety and health standards.

In 2014 the Afghan government published a list of 19 hazardous occupations prohibited for children. These jobs include carpet weaving, metal work, and brick making. Children working in the carpet sector, for example, face physical injury such as carpal tunnel syndrome, neuralgia, and swollen finger joints from long hours sitting at the loom and performing repetitive motions with sharp equipment. They also risk eye strain from close work in poor lighting, and respiratory problems from inhaling fine wool dust. Children employed in brick kilns also risk respiratory illnesses and heat stroke. Children working in the metal industry are exposed to dangers such as cuts and burns from welding and cutting sheet metal.

Multiple wars have ravaged Afghanistan. Rivers are poisoned, irrigation systems ruined, and livestock depleted. Education and health care systems have collapsed. Afghans throughout the country have faced steadily rising unemployment while regular attacks and explosions have forced many hundreds to flee their homes each week. Thousands of Afghan families poured meagre savings into helping at least one member flee the country. An estimated 213,000 Afghan people made it to Europe in 2015. Some 2.7 million Afghans have been exiled for decades. In Pakistan 1.6 million found shelter and 950,000 fled to Iran. Now, Afghans in Europe, Pakistan and Iran are being pushed back into Afghanistan. They must join the 1.8 million people who are already internally displaced refugees.

At a time when Afghan refugees most need compassion, they are among the millions being told to go back where they came from, even if they face death and destitution upon return. In coming months, Afghanistan's internally displaced refugee population is likely to double, with estimates that as many as three million people will be living in tent-like shelters. Bracing themselves for a cold winter, many will lack fuel, blankets, food, jobs and potable water. Already, Afghanistan has the highest rate of infant mortality in the world – 112 deaths for every 1,000 births; 97,000 children suffer from severe acute malnutrition. The children in refugee camps who do survive often become their family's main income earner.

Today, around the world, is Armistice Day. The day originally commemorated the end of the nightmare that was the First World War. Following that slaughter, the US and 80 other countries ultimately ratified the Kellogg–Briand pact, which outlawed war. It would be near the end of the Korean War that Republican President Dwight Eisenhower would issue his 'Chance for Peace' address, saying:

> Every gun that is made, every warship launched, every rocket fired signifies, in the final sense, a theft from those who hunger and are not fed, those who are cold and are not clothed. This world in arms is not spending money alone. It is spending the sweat of its laborers, the genius of its scientists, the hopes of its children.

In a winter seemingly robbed of hope, as the Standing Rock protesters dig in to defend their shore of the Missouri river, we can't switch on a news programme without wading in what seems a poisoned river; so many fictions uttered that it's tempting not to even try refuting them, just tally them. We in the US witness rebellions from various sides of our cultural divisions while many urgent causes which this historical moment brings are completely ignored, not to be discussed. Afghanistan is not discussed. Our patterns of consumption, militarism and pollution continue to devastate our battered environment, but relationships between militarism and climate change are barely researched. We in the US could assume responsibility for the suffering US wars have caused. We could pay reparations to those whose lives have been forever altered by US arrogance and the horror that is war. Instead the US government finds itself beholden to weapon makers and military contractors, bankers and energy magnates, as well as campaign donors who constrict the official discussion in every election to a maddening choice between rival desperations, with more war always the consequence.

On this Armistice Day, we face the troubling fact that US/NATO plans for bases and military exercises call for spending on the Pentagon's 'European Reassurance Initiative' to quadruple, climbing from $789 million in 2016 to $3.4 billion in 2017. Much of this additional funding will go to the deployment of an additional armoured-brigade combat team in northern Europe. World wars have caused much darker days before. People in comparatively wealthy areas of the world may be spared future days of comparable horror.

But there is a peace treaty that needs to be established *between* all US people who would rather not see their children sent off to war in Iraq or Syria or Russia, who would rather not see the earth reduced to ashes and their children to penury at the whims of the well-connected and the mighty. And there is an urgently-needed peace to be forged *between* the US and the refugees of our US and NATO war-making overseas, even as we resolve to end further violence and pay reparations so that displaced people can live dignified lives with the hope of one day returning to their homes.

Many US people awoke this week with a new understanding of the dangers facing our common life together. These battles we fight are not a game, and they can escalate into even more dire realities. I look to Afghanistan, I look to the simple facts faced by the Standing Rock protesters, and I know we must look back to the sorrows which so much of the world will commemorate today. These sorrows, so painfully real, can help all of us yearn above all for an understanding by people worldwide, and here in my own frightened, divided country — an understanding that we live in a real world, beset with multiple wars and must at last turn to each other, prepared to live more simply, share resources more radically, and abolish all wars in order to build a real peace.

Redefining 'Imminent': How the US Department of Justice Makes Murder Respectable, Kills the Innocent and Jails their Defenders

Brian Terrell

November 2014

On 7 October, thirteen years to the day from the beginning of 'Operation Enduring Freedom', Kathy Kelly of Voices for Creative Nonviolence and Georgia Walker, an activist in Kansas City, were arraigned in US District Court in Jefferson City, Missouri. They were summoned to answer charges that they trespassed at Whiteman Air Force Base during a protest against war crimes and assassinations carried out from that base using remotely-controlled drone aircraft.

This is the same court that in 2012 sentenced me to six months in prison, Mark Kenney to four months and Ron Faust to five years' probation. Judge Whitworth explained our convictions and the severity of these sentences telling us that he was responsible for the security of the B-2 'Spirit' Stealth Bomber, also based at Whiteman. The B-2 was never mentioned during our trial, only after we were found guilty, and the airmen of the Air Force police brought to witness against us testified that we had posed no danger to the security of the base or to the weapons housed there. As a US Magistrate, the Judge was sworn to rule by law, regardless of feelings of responsibility for any particular weapons system; but this, he explained, was a deciding factor ruling against us.

From the Wikipedia entry for Whiteman Air Force Base:

> Whiteman AFB is the only permanent base for the B-2 Spirit stealth bomber. Whiteman can launch combat sorties directly from Missouri to any part of the globe, engaging adversaries with nuclear or conventional weapon payloads. The 509th Bomb Wing first flew the B-2 in combat against Serbia in March 1999. Later, Whiteman B-2s led the way for America's military response to the terrorist attacks on New York and Washington D.C. in September 2001. B-2 bombers were the first U.S. aircraft to enter Afghanistan airspace in October 2001, paving the way for other coalition aircraft to engage Taliban and Al Queda forces [sic]. During these operations, the aircraft flew round-trip from Missouri, logging combat missions in excess of 40 hours — the longest on record.

The first bombs exploded over Kabul on 7 October 2001, so Kathy and Georgia have a significant date to be in court! The B-2 needs in-flight refuelling every six hours and it costs $55,000 an hour just to keep it in the air, not to mention the cost of munitions. The flyers who took the first bombs to Afghanistan were in the air for more than 40 hours straight! Today flying drones at computer terminals, airmen from Whiteman can bomb Afghanistan without missing a coffee break; they can sleep in their own beds. The killing in Afghanistan continues from Whiteman on the cheap for the government, but the costs to people on the ground, here as in Afghanistan and in the ever broadening war of terror, is still exorbitant and dire.

Political language can be used, George Orwell said in 1946, 'to make lies sound truthful and murder respectable, and to give an appearance of solidity to pure wind'. In order to justify its global assassination programme, the Obama administration has had to stretch words beyond their natural breaking points. For instance, any male 14 years or older found dead in a drone strike zone is a 'combatant' unless there is explicit intelligence posthumously proving him innocent. We are also informed that the constitutional guarantee of 'due process' does not imply that the government must precede an execution with a trial. I think the one word most degraded and twisted these days, to the goriest ends, is the word 'imminent'.

Redefining International Law

Just what constitutes an 'imminent' threat? Our government has long taken bold advantage of the American public's willingness to support lavish spending on armaments and to accept civilian casualties in military adventures abroad and depletion of domestic programmes at home, when told these are necessary responses to deflect precisely such threats. The government has vastly expanded the meaning of the word 'imminent'. This new definition is crucial to the US drone programme, designed for projecting lethal force throughout the world. It provides a legal and moral pretext for the annihilation of people far away who pose no real threat to us at all.

The use of armed remotely controlled drones as the United States' favoured weapon in its 'war on terror' is increasing exponentially in recent years, raising many disturbing questions. Wielding 500 pound bombs and Hellfire missiles,

Predator and Reaper drones are not the precise and surgical instruments of war so effusively praised by President Obama for 'narrowly targeting our action against those who want to kill us and not the people they hide among'. It is widely acknowledged that the majority of those killed in drone attacks are unintended, 'collateral' victims. The deaths of the drones' intended targets and how they are chosen should be no less troubling.

Those deliberately targeted by drones are often far from conflict zones, often they are in countries with whom the US is not at war and on some occasions have been US citizens. They are rarely 'taken out' in the heat of battle or while engaged in hostile actions and are more likely to be killed (with anyone in their vicinity) at a wedding, at a funeral, at work, hoeing in the garden, driving down the highway or enjoying a meal with family and friends. These deaths are counted as something other than murder only for the curious insistence by the government's lawyers that each of these victims represent an 'imminent' threat to our lives and safety here at home in the US.

In February 2013, a US Department of Justice White Paper, 'Lawfulness of a Lethal Operation Directed Against a US Citizen Who Is a Senior Operational Leader of Al-Qaeda or an Associated Force', was leaked by NBC News. This paper sheds some light on the legal justification for drone assassinations and explains the new and more flexible definition of the word 'imminent'. 'First', it declares, 'the condition that an operational leader presents an "imminent" threat of violent attack against the United States does not require the United States to have clear evidence that a specific attack on U.S. persons and interests will take place in the immediate future'.

Before the Department of Justice lawyers got a hold of it, the meaning of the word 'imminent' was unmistakably clear. Various dictionaries of the English language are all in agreement that the word 'imminent' explicitly denotes something definite and immediate, 'likely to occur at any moment', 'impending', 'ready to take place', 'looming', 'pending', 'threatening', 'around the corner'. Nor has the legal definition of the word left room for ambiguity. After World War II, the Nuremberg Tribunal reaffirmed a 19th-century formulation of customary international law written by Daniel Webster, which said that the necessity for preemptive use of force in self-defence must be 'instant, overwhelming, and leaving no choice of means, and no moment for deliberation'. That was in the past. Now, any possible future threat – and any person on earth arguably might pose one – however remote, can satisfy the new definition. As far as the Justice Department is concerned, an 'imminent' threat is now whomever an 'informed high-level U.S. government official' determines to be such, based on evidence known to that official alone, never to be made public or reviewed by any court.

The Creech 14

The breadth of the government's definition of 'imminent' is murderous in its enormity. It is all the more ironic that the same Department of Justice will also regularly define the word so narrowly as to convict and imprison law abiding and responsible citizens who act to defend the innocent from genuinely imminent harm by the actions of the US government. One example especially relevant to the issue of killing by drone is the case of the 'Creech 14'.

After the first act of nonviolent resistance to the lethal use of unmanned and remotely controlled drones in the United States took place at Creech Air Force Base in Nevada back in April 2009, it took more than a year before the fourteen of us accused of criminal trespass had our day in court. As this was the first opportunity for activists to 'put drones on trial' at a time when few Americans were aware they even existed, we were especially diligent in preparing our case, to argue clearly and cogently, not in order to keep ourselves out of jail but for the sake of those who have died and those who live in fear of the drones. With coaching by some fine trial lawyers, our intention was to represent ourselves and, drawing on humanitarian international law, to offer a strong defence of necessity, even while we were aware that there was little chance that the court would hear our arguments.

The defence of necessity, that one has not committed a crime if an act that is otherwise illegal was done to prevent a greater harm or crime from being perpetrated, is recognized by the Supreme Court as a part of the common law. It is not an exotic or even a particularly unusual defence. 'The rationale behind the necessity defence is that sometimes, in a particular situation, a technical breach of the law is more advantageous to society than the consequence of strict adherence to the law', says West's *Encyclopedia of American Law*. 'The defense is often used successfully in cases that involve a Trespass on property to save a person's life or property.' It might appear, then, that this defence is a natural one for minor infractions such as our alleged trespass, intended to stop the use of drones in a war of aggression, the crime against peace that the Nuremberg Tribunal named 'the supreme international crime'.

In reality, though, courts in the US almost never allow the

necessity defence to be raised in cases like ours. Most of us were experienced enough not to be surprised when we finally got to the Justice Court in Las Vegas in September 2010, and Judge Jensen ruled in lockstep with his judicial colleagues. He insisted at the onset of our case that he was having none of it. 'Go ahead', he said, allowing us to call our expert witnesses but sternly forbidding us from asking them any questions that matter. 'Understand, it is only going to be limited to trespass, what knowledge he or she has, if any, whether you were or were not out at the base. We're not getting into international laws; that's not the issue. That's not the issue. What the government is doing wrong, that's not the issue. The issue is trespass.'

Our co-defendant Steve Kelly followed the judge's instructions and questioned our first witness, former US Attorney General Ramsey Clark, about his firsthand knowledge of trespass laws from working at the Department of Justice during the Kennedy and Johnson administrations. Steve specifically guided the witness to speak of 'the cases of trespass ... of lunch counter activities where laws stated you were not to sit at certain lunch counters' in the struggle for civil rights. Ramsey Clark acknowledged that those arrested for violating these laws had not committed crimes. Steve pushed his luck with the judge and offered the classic illustration of the necessity defence: 'A situation where there is a "no trespassing" sign and there is smoke coming out of a door or a window and a person is up on the upper floor in need of help. To enter that building, in a real narrow technical sense, would be trespass. Is there a possibility, in the long run, it wouldn't be trespass to help the person upstairs?' Ramsey replied, 'We would hope so, wouldn't we? To have a baby burn to death or something, because of a "no trespass" sign would be poor public policy to put it mildly. Criminal.'

Judge Jensen by this time was obviously intrigued. His ruling to limit the testimony to trespass held, but as his fascination grew, so his interpretation of his own order grew more elastic. Over the repeated objections of the prosecution team, the judge allowed limited but powerful testimony from Ramsey and our other witnesses, retired US Army Colonel and former diplomat Ann Wright and Loyola Law School Professor Bill Quigley, that put our alleged trespass into its context as an act to stop a heinous crime.

I had the honour of making the closing statement for the accused, which I ended with, 'We fourteen are the ones who are seeing the smoke from the burning house and we are not going to be stopped by a "no trespassing" sign from going to the burning children'.

Our appreciation for a judge's extraordinary attention to the facts of the case aside, we still expected nothing but an immediate conviction and sentencing. Judge Jensen surprised us: 'I consider it more than just a plain trespass trial. A lot of serious issues are at stake here. So I'm going to take it under advisement and I will render a written decision. And it may take me two to three months to do so, because I want to make sure that I'm right on whatever I rule on.'

When we returned to Las Vegas in January 2011, Judge Jensen read his decision that it was just a plain trespass trial after all and we were guilty. Among several justifications for convicting us, the judge rejected what he called 'the Defendants' claim of necessity' because 'first, the Defendants failed to show that their protest was designed to prevent "imminent" harm'. He faulted our case for not presenting the court with 'evidence that any military activities involving drones were being conducted or about to be conducted on the day of the Defendants' arrest', seeming to forget that he had ordered us not to submit any such evidence, even if we had it.

Judge Jensen's verdict was amply supported by the precedents he cited, including a 1991 appellate court ruling, *US v Schoon*, that concerned a protest aimed to 'keep US tax dollars out of El Salvador' at an IRS office in Tucson. In this protest, the Ninth Circuit ruled, 'the requisite imminence was lacking'. In other words, because the harm protested was taking place in El Salvador, a trespass in Tucson cannot be justified. So, Judge Jensen reasoned, burning children in a house in Afghanistan cannot excuse a trespass in Nevada.

We are all Potential Targets
The NBC leak of that Department of Justice White Paper wouldn't happen for two more years (call it suppression of evidence?) and as far as Judge Jensen knew, the dictionary definition of 'imminent' was still operant. Even so, had we been allowed to testify beyond the narrow confines set at trial, we would have shown that, with new satellite technology, the lethal threat we were addressing there is always imminent by any reasonable definition of the word. Although the victims of drone violence on the day of our arrest were indeed far away in Afghanistan and Iraq, those crimes were actually being committed by combatants sitting at computer screens, engaged in real-time hostilities in trailers on the base, not so far at all from where we were apprehended by Air Force police.

The government does not believe that it needs to have 'clear evidence that a specific attack on U.S. persons and interests will take place in the immediate future' to establish an imminent threat and so carry out extrajudicial executions of human beings anywhere on the planet. Citizens who act to stop killing by drones, on the other hand, are required to have specific 'evidence that any military activities involving drones were being conducted or about to be conducted', in order to justify nonviolently entering into government property. The government's position on this lacks coherence, at best. Even after the publication of its White Paper, the Department of Justice continues to block defendants accused of trespass from even mentioning the fact that they were arrested while responding to an imminent threat to innocent life, and the courts obligingly accept this contradiction.

The defence of necessity does not simply justify actions that technically violate the law. 'Necessity', says West's *Encyclopedia of American Law*, is 'a defense asserted by a criminal or civil defendant that he or she had no choice but to break the law'. As Ramsey Clark testified in a Las Vegas courtroom five years ago, 'to have a baby burn to death because of a "no trespass" sign would be poor public policy to put it mildly'. In a time of burning children, the 'no trespassing' signs attached to the fences that protect the crimes executed with drones and other instruments of terror hold no potency and they do not command our obedience. The courts that do not recognize this reality allow themselves to be used as instruments of governmental malfeasance.

There have been many more trials since the Creech 14 and, in the meanwhile, many more children have been incinerated by missiles fired from drones. On 10 December, International Human Rights Day, Georgia Walker and Kathy Kelly will go to trial in US District Court in Jefferson City, Missouri, after they peacefully brought their grievance and a loaf of bread onto Whiteman Air Force Base, another in the growing number of stateside remote control killer drone centres.

Two years ago in that same court in a similar case, Judge Whitworth rejected the necessity defence offered by Ron Faust and me, subsequently sentencing Ron to five years of probation and sending me to prison for six months. It is to be hoped that Judge Whitworth will take advantage of this second chance that Kathy and Georgia courageously offer and exonerate himself and his profession.

America – and why Britain sucks up to it...

Robin Ramsay

March 2009

Below is the text of a talk I was supposed to give at Hull University – but didn't. For reasons unknown the event was cancelled. Since the arrangements were done by email and I didn't meet the man organizing it, nor know his full name, if he continues to ignore my emails I may never find out why the plug was pulled. When discussing what I would talk about I suggested I write something and send it to him. His initial reaction to reading it was 'Terrific' but then communication ceased. My guess is that someone in his department – he's a student doing War and Security Studies, and such departments are never a million miles from the Ministry of Defence, even if they aren't funded by it – took offence at my proposed text.

I was a student here from 1971-74 doing a social science degree; but more importantly, between 1976 and 1982 I was on the dole much of the time and spent most of my days in the library here, educating myself in post-war history, American history, what was available then about the intelligence services – almost nothing – and the post-WW2 geopolitical order; centrally the Cold War and American imperialism. Looking at the reading list for the intelligence and national security component of this course, what struck me was that almost none of its literature existed when I was here. As an academic subject, most of this course is recent. I have read a few of the books on the list and none of the academic articles. What could I say on a subject of whose content I have read so little?

I have done what anybody would do: I looked at the literature and found a way to use it as a platform for something I am interested in. And that is this country's relationship with the United States: because that relationship is one of the central features of this course, although it is probably never stated as such. (I may be wrong about this: I have only seen a sketch of the course content.) Britain's military, intelligence and foreign policy organizations are more or less integrated into and subservient to their American counterparts. In boxing-weight terms we are talking about a British flyweight and an American super heavyweight.

From the American point of view, Britain has been useful first as being what George Orwell called Airstrip One in the 1940s and Duncan Campbell called the unsinkable aircraft carrier in the 1980s, for the US Air Force. Secondly, after the early 1960s when US banks began moving their money out of America to avoid taxation and President Kennedy's attempts to regulate their activities, Britain became the offshore banking centre of choice for Wall Street. And thirdly, Britain has been useful as diplomatic cover for American power. For 60 years Britain has 'stood by' its ally, through the slaughter in Vietnam, half a million dead Indonesians, military coups all over south America in the '60s and '70s, hundreds of thousands of deaths in Guatemala, El Salvador and Nicaragua in the 1980s, right up to supporting it while it killed somewhere between half a million and a million Iraqis. Britain has been a bomber base, a tax avoidance

AMERICA – AND WHY BRITAIN SUCKS UP TO IT... | 73

centre for US banks and a diplomatic fig leaf of 'international support'.

In 1962 Dean Acheson, who had been US Secretary of State from 1949–53, when the post-WW2 order was being built, said that Britain 'has lost an empire and has not yet found a role'. This is always quoted as being a great profundity. In fact it was just nonsense. In 1945 America became the new school bully and after Suez, Britain became the school bully's best friend. That has been this country's chief international role. Being the bully's friend has its upside – you don't get hit – but it is basically a degrading role, characterized by public grovelling and private bad-mouthing. Which is what the Brits do to the Americans: they say nothing in public until the Americans fuck-up and then they mutter in the corner about the dumb, incompetent, cowboy Yanks, as they did most recently over the debacle in Iraq.

You may be thinking that I am anti-American. Not so: but I am anti-American foreign policy. America as a country is wonderful in many ways. Almost all of the culture which influenced me growing up in the '60s and '70s – books, movies, music – was American. But not straight white bread, American. Not *Time* magazine, suburban, button-down, American. My heroes were black or beats, or musicians: Jazz, R & B, blues. Mailer, Baldwin, Kerouac, Ginsberg. John Lee Hooker, Buddy Guy, Miles Davis, John Coltrane. The other America.

I have done the great American road trip three times: rented cars and just driven. In total, my partner and I have spent eight weeks driving round rural America, staying in motels, eating in diners and drinking in the nearest bars.

The Americans you meet while doing this are exactly the

friendly, open people the books tell you about. But the Americans you meet in a bar out in Carrizozo, New Mexico or Sundance, Wyoming, mostly know nothing about and care nothing about American foreign policy. Indeed, most of them know nothing about and care nothing about foreign *anything*. The last time I saw a figure, only 13% of Americans had a passport. In American bars you cannot discuss American history (because the locals know little and what they do know is generally nonsense), American politics (ditto) and American foreign policy (ditto). (But then this would be true of peasants anywhere, and in rural America what you are meeting are essentially peasants.)

After 9/11 there was a number one hit song by one of America's country music stars, Alan Jackson, which included the lines, 'I watch CNN but I'm not sure I can tell you/The difference between Iraq and Iran'; and I'm sure he and the vast majority of the white Americans who bought the single or heard it on the radio didn't know the difference. And didn't care. Of course the Bush administration used this ignorance to attack Iraq while hinting that Iraq was behind 9/11. Never mind that Iraq was a secular national socialist state and Bin Laden a fundamentalist Muslim. Who knew that, out there in backwoods South Dakota, right?

I have always been anti-American foreign policy. My parents were in the Communist Party until the Soviet invasion of Hungary in 1956; and I grew up in a climate in which the instinctive reaction to any foreign policy issue was: the Soviets are right and the Americans are wrong. It took me until I was well into my twenties to shed that instinctive pro-Soviet reaction. But the other half of the reaction, the anti-American one, I have not shed. Because it is correct: the

AMERICA – AND WHY BRITAIN SUCKS UP TO IT... | 75

Americans were usually in the wrong. In part this is axiomatic: imperialism is always wrong. In my view good imperialism is a contradiction in terms. The historical truth is that since WW2, when America became the world's dominant power, apart from the famine in China in the late 1950s, most of the corpses in this period have been created by America, its allies, its proxies, or as a result of America's meddling in the politics of other societies. Difficult though this is to grasp for those of us living in this little island, after 1945 the US set out to monitor, surveil and, where necessary, regulate the entire non-communist world.

Because the UK and the US are allies, these simple historical facts are excluded from this society's public understanding of the world, its public discourse, if you like. And, I would guess, it is excluded from courses such as this one. A module titled 'British defence and security policy's role in supporting global slaughter, subversion and terror' – which is what US foreign policy has largely been about since WW2 – is not a module you will find in many British universities. People who talk like this do not often get invited onto *Newsnight*. To talk as I am doing is to be 'an extremist'.

All of which raises the obvious question: why have this country's political, media, military and intelligence elites supported the path of subservience, of being America's flunkeys. A number of factors are visible, though how you would calculate their relative weight I don't know.

First, there is the mutual history. Less than a hundred years ago the American foreign policy establishment and the British foreign policy establishment were interlinked through a set of networks created after WW1: the British end was the elaborated Round Table network, the American end the Council on

Foreign Relations. This is the origins of the so-called 'special relationship'. While these networks declined in significance in the 1930s, the Anglo-American link was renewed during WW2 and carried on into the Cold War years and the creation of NATO under US leadership.

Second, as the British armed forces have not been powerful enough since the end of the Second World War to defend the international capitalist order in which British overseas investments are located, the British state tagged along with the Americans who did have the muscle to police the non-communist world. This is even more true now than it was in, say, the late 1950s.

Third, as the US developed global electronic surveillance systems which the British state could not match, our secret servants came to rely on US-generated intelligence.

The fourth reason the UK is subservient to the US, is that a large part of the City of London is now owned by American banks — banks which British politicians have been afraid to regulate lest they unplug their computers and take them elsewhere. This may change as the current crisis unravels.

And fifthly, and this may now be the most important factor of all, British state personnel and politicians individually benefit from the link with the Americans.

Here is the late Hugo Young's notes on a conversation with the late Robin Cook, when Cook was Foreign Secretary in the first Blair administration. Young asked Cook why the British government supports the US so slavishly.

Because of the Ministry of Defence's fanatical determination to keep close to the Pentagon. They will never do anything that puts that relationship out of line. The truth is that it is the pivot of all military careers and a great deal of decision-making. Any military officer who has ambitions, has to keep close to the Pentagon, because he needs to serve in NATO. The US and the UK have dominated serious appointments in NATO for years, for this reason. It is the driving priority of the MOD to keep it that way. They do not think in terms of national interest, but of both MOD interest and the American interest.

And talking about the bombing during the war after the break-up of Yugoslavia, Young comments:

> Cook ... always had to be asked for target approval for each new bombing raid. Sometimes he tried to say no. Each time the MOD pleaded the terrible consequence of displeasing the USA. From the USA's point of view, we gave them cover. They could always say we were doing it too.

The striking thing to me is how banal this is. There is no theory of the world here. If you are a British general, diplomat, politician, by virtue of being America's gopher, you get to hang around the top table and play with the big boys in a way that — say — their Italian equivalents never do.

You may have noticed that the stick the Americans wave at British politicians who look like they might disobey US instructions or create embarrassment is the threat of cutting the Brits off from the US intelligence feed. Now, what the British state can actually do with this intelligence, we don't know. Given the toy-town nature of our armed forces these days — the Royal Navy has more admirals than ships for example — my guess would be, not very much. The British armed forces today could not, for example, re-fight the 1982 war with Argentina: there are not enough British-flagged ships left to transport the troops and material to the South Atlantic.

To my knowledge, since Suez in 1956 the British state has refused only twice to do what the Americans wanted. In <u>1965–66 Harold Wilson refused to send British troops to Vietnam</u>, despite heavy pressure from President Johnson and threats to halt US support for sterling. (This was back in the days when currencies had fixed exchange rates and states had to spend their reserves, if necessary, defending that rate.) Wilson refused for two reasons that I am aware of. The most pressing was that had he sent UK troops to Vietnam there would have been massive problems with the left-wing of the Labour Party in and outside parliament. And in those days this mattered. The second reason was suggested by the former SIS officer Anthony Cavendish, who told me twenty years ago that Maurice Oldfield, when deputy chief of SIS, had warned Wilson not to get embroiled in Vietnam. Oldfield had served as an SIS regional head in the Far East in the middle 1950s when the French were driven out of Vietnam and seems to have acquired a more rational appreciation of the situation there than the Americans did.

After 1966 the counter-intelligence section of the CIA, headed by the loony James Angleton, came to believe that Prime Minister Harold Wilson was a Soviet agent; and CIA counterintelligence was the ultimate source of much of the disinformation and smears about him and those around him in the middle 1970s. This may have been payback for Wilson's temerity in refusing to bend.

It is said, by Professor Richard Aldrich amongst others, that in 1973 Prime Minister <u>Edward Heath refused to allow the</u>

Americans to use British bases in Cyprus for intelligence gathering during the Yom Kippur war between Israel and some of its Arab neighbours; and that this resulted in a temporary halt in the US signals intelligence flow to the UK.

Heath was defeated two years later in a leadership contest by Margaret Thatcher, whom the Americans had been cultivating and promoting since 1967 as a potential leader of the Conservative Party. (And we know this from declassified State Department files.) This may have been payback for Heath daring to defy the Americans.

Is Britain then just an American colony? Not in any conventional sense of colony. At any rate, if we have been colonized, we have done it to ourselves. But if we ask how much independence the UK government has, the answer has to be that I don't know. The British state apparently gets most of its intelligence from the US and most of its weapons systems, notably its nuclear weapons, which are also controlled by the US.

The day I wrote some of this a former British intelligence officer, Crispin Black, wrote in *The Independent on Sunday* of the 'special relationship syndrome' which affects British politicians and state officials and noted that:

> The Joint Intelligence Committee, the military, the intelligence services, the mechanisms that control our 'independent' nuclear deterrent are all heavily 'penetrated' by American influence. It is almost impossible for a British minister to make a decision on a range of national security and foreign policy subjects without the US being involved at every level. The UK's national security infrastructure runs on US software which we have happily installed.

The UK's economic independence is constrained by its membership of the World Trade Organization and IMF, both controlled by the Americans, and by the demands of the City of London, now largely owned by American banks. Most of our popular culture is imported from America, along with the central economic and cultural concepts which are in our politicians' heads: no bigger fans of all things American have there been than Messieurs Brown and Blair following in the footsteps of Margaret Thatcher. Brown and Blair, like Thatcher, enjoyed several freebie trips to the US from the US State Department while they were rising politicians.

Since Suez in 1956, no UK government has ever tried to find out how much real independence we have. The curious thing to me in all this is how little political interest there is in this. We have UKIP, the United Kingdom Independence Party — but does it refer to freedom from America? Not that I can see. It is solely focused on the EU. And, with the exception of a handful on the Labour left, an even smaller handful on the left of the Lib-Dems, and a few on the Tory right, there are no MPs that I am aware of who are pursuing this.

In this society, influence can often be measured by the amount of media noise being created. But it can also be measured by the silence around certain subjects. By that standard, subservience to America is one of our society's great no-go areas.

The Enemy is Not Trump, it is Ourselves

John Pilger

January 2017

On the day President Trump is inaugurated, thousands of writers in the United States expressed their indignation. 'In order for us to heal and move forward...', say Writers Resist, 'we wish to bypass direct political discourse, in favour of an inspired focus on the future, and how we, as writers, can be a unifying force for the protection of democracy'.

And: 'We urge local organizers and speakers to avoid using the names of politicians or adopting "anti" language as the focus for their Writers Resist event. It's important to ensure that nonprofit organizations, which are prohibited from political campaigning, will feel confident participating in and sponsoring these events.'

Thus, real protest is to be avoided, for it is not tax exempt.

Compare such drivel with the declarations of the Congress of American Writers, held at Carnegie Hall, New York, in 1935, and again two years later. They were electric events, with writers discussing how they could confront ominous events in Abyssinia, China and Spain. Telegrams from Thomas Mann, C. Day Lewis, Upton Sinclair and Albert Einstein were read out, reflecting the fear that great power was now rampant and that it had become impossible to discuss art and literature without politics or, indeed, direct political action.

'A writer', the journalist Martha Gellhorn told the second congress, 'must be a man of action now... A man who has given a year of his life to steel strikes, or to the unemployed, or to the problems of racial prejudice, has not lost or wasted time. He is a man who has known where he belonged. If you should survive such action, what you have to say about it afterwards is the truth, is necessary and real, and it will last.'

Her words echo across the unction and violence of the Obama era and the silence of those who colluded with his deceptions.

That the menace of rapacious power – rampant long before the rise of Trump – has been accepted by writers, many of them privileged and celebrated, and by those who guard the gates of literary criticism, and culture, including popular culture, is uncontroversial. Not for them the impossibility of writing and promoting literature bereft of politics. Not for them the responsibility to speak out, regardless of who occupies the White House.

Today, false symbolism is all. 'Identity' is all. In 2016, Hillary Clinton stigmatized millions of voters as 'a basket of deplorables, racist, sexist, homophobic, xenophobic, Islamaphobic – you name it'. Her abuse was handed out at an LGBT rally as part of her cynical campaign to win over minorities by abusing a white mostly working-class majority. Divide and rule, this is called; or identity politics in which race and gender conceal class, and allow the waging of class war. Trump understood this.

'When the truth is replaced by silence', said the Soviet dissident poet Yevtushenko, 'the silence is a lie'.

This is not an American phenomenon. A few years ago,

THE ENEMY IS NOT TRUMP, IT IS OURSELVES | 83

Terry Eagleton, then professor of English literature at Manchester University, reckoned that 'for the first time in two centuries, there is no eminent British poet, playwright or novelist prepared to question the foundations of the western way of life'.

No Shelley speaks for the poor, no Blake for utopian dreams, no Byron damns the corruption of the ruling class, no Thomas Carlyle and John Ruskin reveal the moral disaster of capitalism. William Morris, Oscar Wilde, HG Wells, George Bernard Shaw have no equivalents today. Harold Pinter was the last to raise his voice. Among today's insistent voices of consumer-feminism, none echoes Virginia Woolf, who described 'the arts of dominating other people ... of ruling, of killing, of acquiring land and capital'.

There is something both venal and profoundly stupid about famous writers as they venture outside their cosseted world and embrace an 'issue'. Across the Review section of the *Guardian* on 10 December was a dreamy picture of Barack Obama looking up to the heavens and the words, 'Amazing Grace' and 'Farewell the Chief'.

The sycophancy ran like a polluted babbling brook through page after page. 'He was a vulnerable figure in many ways ... But the grace. The all-encompassing grace: in manner and form, in argument and intellect, with humour and cool ... [He] is a blazing tribute to what has been, and what can be again ... He seems ready to keep fighting, and remains a formidable champion to have on our side ... The grace ... the almost surreal levels of grace ...'

I have conflated these quotes. There are others even more hagiographic and bereft of mitigation. The *Guardian*'s chief apologist for Obama, Gary Younge, has always been careful to mitigate, to say that his hero 'could have done more': oh, but there were the 'calm, measured and consensual solutions...'

None of them, however, could surpass the American writer, Ta-Nehisi Coates, the recipient of a 'genius' grant worth $625,000 from a liberal foundation. In an interminable essay for *The Atlantic* entitled, 'My President Was Black', Coates brought new meaning to prostration. The final 'chapter', entitled 'When You Left, You Took All of Me With You', a line from a Marvin Gaye song, describes seeing the Obamas' 'rising out of the limo, rising up from fear, smiling, waving, defying despair, defying history, defying gravity'. The Ascension, no less.

One of the persistent strands in American political life is a cultish extremism that approaches fascism. This was given expression and reinforced during the two terms of Barack Obama. 'I believe in American exceptionalism with every fibre of my being', said Obama, who expanded America's favourite military pastime, bombing, and death squads ('special operations') as no other president has done since the Cold War.

According to a Council on Foreign Relations survey, in 2016 alone Obama dropped 26,171 bombs. That is 72 bombs every day. He bombed the poorest people on earth, in Afghanistan, Libya, Yemen, Somalia, Syria, Iraq, Pakistan.

Every Tuesday – reported the *New York Times* – he personally selected those who would be murdered by mostly hellfire missiles fired from drones. Weddings, funerals, shepherds were attacked, along with those attempting to collect the body parts festooning the 'terrorist target'. A leading Republican senator, Lindsey Graham, estimated,

THE ENEMY IS NOT TRUMP, IT IS OURSELVES | 85

approvingly, that Obama's drones killed 4,700 people. 'Sometimes you hit innocent people and I hate that', he said, 'but we've taken out some very senior members of Al-Qaeda'.

Like the fascism of the 1930s, big lies are delivered with the precision of a metronome, thanks to an omnipresent media whose description now fits that of the Nuremberg prosecutor: 'Before each major aggression, with some few exceptions based on expediency, they initiated a press campaign calculated to weaken their victims and to prepare the German people psychologically... In the propaganda system... it was the daily press and the radio that were the most important weapons'.

Take the catastrophe in Libya. In 2011, Obama said Libyan president Muammar Gaddafi was planning 'genocide' against his own people. 'We knew... that if we waited one more day, Benghazi, a city the size of Charlotte [North Carolina], could suffer a massacre that would have reverberated across the region and stained the conscience of the world.'

This was the known lie of Islamist militias facing defeat by Libyan government forces. It became the media story; and NATO – led by Obama and Hillary Clinton – launched 9,700 'strike sorties' against Libya, of which more than a third were aimed at civilian targets. Uranium warheads were used; the cities of Misrata and Sirte were carpet-bombed. The Red Cross identified mass graves, and Unicef reported that 'most [of the children killed] were under the age of ten'.

Under Obama, the US has extended secret 'special forces' operations to 138 countries, or 70 per cent of the world's population. The first African-American president launched what amounted to a full-scale invasion of Africa. Reminiscent of the Scramble for Africa in the late 19th century, the US African Command (Africom) has built a network of suppliants among collaborative African regimes eager for American bribes and armaments. Africom's 'soldier to soldier' doctrine embeds US officers at every level of command, from general to warrant officer. Only pith helmets are missing.

It is as if Africa's proud history of liberation, from Patrice Lumumba to Nelson Mandela, is consigned to oblivion by a new master's black colonial elite whose 'historic mission', warned Frantz Fanon half a century ago, is the promotion of 'a capitalism rampant though camouflaged'.

It was Obama who, in 2011, announced what became known as the 'pivot to Asia', in which almost two-thirds of US naval forces would be transferred to the Asia–Pacific to 'confront China', in the words of his Defense Secretary. There was no threat from China; the entire enterprise was unnecessary. It was an extreme provocation to keep the Pentagon and its demented brass happy.

In 2014, Obama's administration oversaw and paid for a fascist-led coup in Ukraine against the democratically-elected government, threatening Russia in the western borderland through which Hitler invaded the Soviet Union, with a loss of 27 million lives. It was Obama who placed missiles in Eastern Europe aimed at Russia, and it was the winner of the Nobel Peace Prize who increased spending on nuclear warheads to a level higher than that of any administration since the Cold War – having promised, in an emotional speech in Prague, to 'help rid the world of nuclear weapons'.

Obama, the constitutional lawyer, prosecuted more whistleblowers than any other president in history, even though the

US Constitution protects them. He declared Chelsea Manning guilty before the end of a trial that was a travesty. Although Manning is to be released in May, Obama has refused to quash the outrageous sentence under which he suffered seven years of inhumane treatment, which the UN said amounted to torture. He has pursued an entirely bogus case against Julian Assange. He promised to close the Guantanamo concentration camp and didn't.

Following the public relations disaster of George W. Bush, Obama, the smooth operator from Chicago via Harvard, was enlisted to restore what he calls 'leadership' throughout the world. The Nobel Prize committee's decision was part of this: the kind of cloying reverse racism that beatified the man for no reason other than he was attractive to liberal sensibilities and, of course, American power, if not to the children he kills in impoverished, mostly Muslim countries.

This is the Call of Obama. It is not unlike a dog whistle: inaudible to most, irresistible to the besotted and boneheaded, especially 'liberal brains pickled in the formaldehyde of identity politics', as Luciana Bohne put it. 'When Obama walks into a room', gushed George Clooney, 'you want to follow him somewhere, anywhere'.

William I. Robinson, professor at the University of California, and one of an uncontaminated group of American strategic thinkers who have retained their independence during the years of intellectual dog-whistling since 9/11, wrote this last week:

> President Barack Obama ... may have done more than anyone to assure [Donald] Trump's victory. While Trump's election has triggered a rapid expansion of fascist currents

in US civil society, a fascist outcome for the political system is far from inevitable.... But that fight back requires clarity as to how we got to such a dangerous precipice. The seeds of 21st century fascism were planted, fertilized and watered by the Obama administration and the politically bankrupt liberal elite.

Robinson points out that,

> whether in its 20th or its emerging 21st century variants, fascism is, above all, a response to deep structural crises of capitalism, such as that of the 1930s and the one that began with the financial meltdown in 2008... There is a near-straight line here from Obama to Trump... The liberal elite's refusal to challenge the rapaciousness of transnational capital and its brand of identity politics served to eclipse the language of the working and popular classes... pushing white workers into an 'identity' of white nationalism and helping the neo-fascists to organise them.

The seedbed is Obama's Weimar Republic, a landscape of endemic poverty, militarized police and barbaric prisons: the consequence of a 'market' extremism which, under his presidency, prompted the transfer of $14 trillion in public money to criminal enterprises in Wall Street.

Perhaps his greatest 'legacy' is the co-option and disorientation of any real opposition. Bernie Sanders' specious 'revolution' does not apply. Propaganda is his triumph.

The lies about Russia – in whose elections the US has openly intervened – have made the world's most self-important journalists laughing stocks. In the country with con-

THE ENEMY IS NOT TRUMP, IT IS OURSELVES

stitutionally the freest press in the world, free journalism now exists only in its honourable exceptions.

The obsession with Trump is a cover for many of those calling themselves 'left/liberal', as if to claim political decency. They are not 'left', neither are they especially 'liberal'. Much of America's aggression towards the rest of humanity has come from so-called liberal Democratic administrations — such as Obama's. America's political spectrum extends from the mythical centre to the lunar right. The 'left' are homeless renegades Martha Gellhorn described as 'a rare and wholly admirable fraternity'. She excluded those who confuse politics with a fixation on their navels.

While they 'heal' and 'move forward', will the Writers Resist campaigners and other anti-Trumpists reflect upon this? More to the point: when will a genuine movement of opposition arise? Angry, eloquent, all-for-one-and-one-for all. Until real politics return to people's lives, the enemy is not Trump, it is ourselves.

Historical Perspective of the 2014 Gaza Massacre

Ilan Pappé

August 2014

People in Gaza and elsewhere in Palestine feel disappointed at the lack of any significant international reaction to the carnage and destruction the Israeli assault has so far left behind it in the Strip. The inability, or unwillingness, to act seems to be first and foremost an acceptance of the Israeli narrative and argumentation for the crisis in Gaza. Israel has developed a very clear narrative about the present carnage in Gaza.

It is a tragedy caused by an unprovoked Hamas missile attack on the Jewish State, to which Israel had to react in self-defence. While mainstream Western media, academia and politicians may have reservations about the proportionality of the force used by Israel, they accept the gist of this argument. This Israeli narrative is totally rejected in the world of cyber activism and alternative media. There, it seems, the condemnation of the Israeli action as a war crime is widespread and consensual.

The main difference between the two analyses from above and from below is the willingness of activists to study deeper and in a more profound way the ideological and historical context of the present Israeli action in Gaza. This tendency should be enhanced even further and this piece is just a modest attempt to contribute towards this direction.

Ad Hoc Slaughter?

An historical evaluation and contextualization of the present Israeli assault on Gaza and that of the previous three ones since 2006 expose clearly the Israeli genocidal policy there. An incremental policy of massive killing that is less a product of a callous intention as it is the inevitable outcome of Israel's overall strategy towards Palestine in general and the areas it occupied in 1967 in particular.

This context should be insisted upon, since the Israeli propaganda machine attempts, again and again, to narrate its policies as out of context, and turns the pretext it found for every new wave of destruction into the main justification for another spree of indiscriminate slaughter in the killing fields of Palestine.

The Israeli strategy of branding its brutal policies as an *ad hoc* response to this or that Palestinian action is as old as the Zionist presence in Palestine itself. It was used repeatedly as a justification for implementing the Zionist vision of a future Palestine that has in it very few, if any, native Palestinians. The means for achieving this goal changed with the years, but the formula has remained the same: whatever the Zionist vision of a Jewish State might be, it can only materialize without any significant number of Palestinians in it. And nowadays the vision is of an Israel stretching over almost the whole of historic Palestine, where millions of Palestinians still live.

This vision ran into trouble once territorial greed led Israel to try and keep the West Bank and the Gaza Strip within its rule and control ever since June 1967. Israel searched for a way to keep the territories it occupied that year without incorporating their population into its rights-bearing citizenry. All the while it participated in a 'peace process' charade to cover up or buy time for its unilateral colonization policies on the ground.

With the decades, Israel differentiated between areas it wished to control directly and those it would manage indirectly, with the aim in the long run of downsizing the Palestinian population to a minimum with, among other means, ethnic cleansing and economic and geographic strangulation. Thus the West Bank was in effect divided into 'Jewish' and 'Palestinian' zones – a reality most Israelis can live with provided the Palestinian Bantustans are content with their incarceration within these mega-prisons. The geopolitical location of the West Bank creates the impression in Israel, at least, that it is possible to achieve this without anticipating a third uprising or too much international condemnation.

The Gaza Strip, due to its unique geopolitical location, did not lend itself that easily to such a strategy. Ever since 1994, and even more so when Ariel Sharon came to power as prime minister in the early 2000s, the strategy there was to ghettoize Gaza and somehow hope that the people there – 1.8 million as of today – would be dropped into eternal oblivion.

But the Ghetto proved to be rebellious and unwilling to live under conditions of strangulation, isolation, starvation and economic collapse. There was no way it would be annexed to Egypt, neither in 1948 nor in 2014. In 1948, Israel pushed into the Gaza area (before it became a strip) hundreds of thousands of refugees it expelled from the northern Naqab and southern coast who, so they hoped, would move even farther away from Palestine.

For a while after 1967, Israel wanted to keep it as a township which provided unskilled labour but without any human and civil rights. When the occupied people resisted the continued oppression in two intifadas, the West Bank was bisected into small Bantustans encircled by Jewish colonies, but it did not work in the too small and too dense Gaza Strip. The Israelis were unable to 'West Bank' the Strip, so to speak. So they cordoned it as a Ghetto, and when it resisted the army was allowed to use its most formidable and lethal weapons to crush it. The inevitable result of an accumulative reaction of this kind was genocidal.

Incremental Genocide

The killing of three Israeli teenagers, two of them minors, abducted in the occupied West Bank in June, which was mainly a reprisal for killings of Palestinian children in May, provided the pretext first and foremost for destroying the delicate unity Hamas and Fatah had formed in that month; a unity that followed a decision by the Palestinian Authority to forsake the 'peace process' and appeal to international organizations to judge Israel according to a human and civil rights' yardstick. Both developments were viewed as alarming in Israel.

The pretext determined the timing – but the viciousness of the assault was the outcome of Israel's inability to formulate a clear policy towards the Strip it created in 1948. The only clear feature of that policy is the deep conviction that wiping out Hamas from the Gaza Strip would domicile the Ghetto there.

Since 1994, even before the rise of Hamas to power in the Gaza Strip, the very particular geopolitical location of the Strip made it clear that any collective punitive action, such as the one inflicted now, could only be an operation of massive killings and destruction. In other words: an incremental genocide.

This recognition never inhibited the generals who give the orders to bomb the people from the air, the sea and the ground. Downsizing the number of Palestinians all over historic Palestine is still the Zionist vision; an ideal that requires the dehumanization of the Palestinians. In Gaza, this attitude and vision take its most inhuman form.

The particular timing of this wave is determined, as in the past, by additional considerations. The domestic social unrest of 2011 is still simmering and for a while there was a public demand to cut military expenditures and move money from the inflated 'defence' budget to social services. The army branded this possibility as suicidal. There is nothing like a military operation to stifle any voices calling on the government to cut its military expenses.

Typical hallmarks of the previous stages in this incremental genocide reappear in this wave as well. As in the first operation against Gaza, 'First Rains' in 2006, and those which followed in 2009, 'Cast Lead', and 2012, 'Pillar of Smoke', one can witness again consensual Israeli–Jewish support for the massacre of civilians in the Gaza Strip, without one significant voice of dissent. Academia, as always, becomes part of the machinery. Various universities offered the state its student bodies to help and battle for the Israeli narrative in cyberspace and the alternative media.

The Israeli media, as well, toed loyally the government's line, showing no pictures of the human catastrophe Israel has wreaked, and informing its public that this time 'the world understands us and is behind us'. That statement is valid to a point as the political elites in the West continue to provide the old immunity to the Jewish state. The recent appeal by Western governments to the prosecutor in the international court of Justice in the Hague not to look into Israel's crimes in Gaza is a case in point. Wide sections of the Western media followed suit and justified, by and large, Israel's actions.

This distorted coverage is also fed by a sense among Western journalists that what happens in Gaza pales in comparison to the atrocities in Iraq and Syria. Comparisons like this are usually provided without a wider historical perspective. A longer view on the history of the Palestinians would be a much more appropriate way to evaluate their suffering *vis-à-vis* the carnage elsewhere.

Conclusion: Confronting Double-standards

But not only is a historical view needed for a better understanding of the massacre in Gaza. A dialectical approach that identifies the connection between Israel's immunity and the horrific developments elsewhere is required as well. The dehumanization in Iraq and Syria is widespread and terrifying, as it is in Gaza. But there is one crucial difference between these cases and the Israeli brutality: the former are condemned as barbarous and inhuman worldwide, while those committed by Israel are still publicly licensed and approved by the president of the United States, the leaders of the EU and Israel's other friends in the world.

The only chance for a successful struggle against Zionism in Palestine is the one based on a human and civil rights agenda that does not differentiate between one violation and the other and yet identifies clearly the victim and the victimizers. Those who commit atrocities in the Arab world against oppressed minorities and helpless communities, as well as the Israelis who commit these crimes against the Palestinian people, should all be judged by the same moral and ethical standards. They are all war criminals, though in the case of Palestine they have been at work longer than anyone else. It does not really matter what the religious identity is of the people who commit the atrocities or in the name of which religion they purport to speak. Whether they call themselves jihadists, Judaists or Zionists, they should be treated in the same way.

A world that would stop employing double standards in its dealings with Israel is a world that could be far more effective in its response to war crimes elsewhere. Cessation of the incremental genocide in Gaza and the restitution of the basic human and civil rights of Palestinians, wherever they are, including the right of return, is the only way to open a new vista for a productive international intervention in the Middle East as a whole.

Terror in Britain: What did the Prime Minister Know?

John Pilger

May 2017

The unsayable in Britain's general election campaign is this. The causes of the Manchester atrocity, in which 22 mostly young people were murdered by a jihadist, are being suppressed to protect the secrets of British foreign policy.

Critical questions – such as why the security service MI5 maintained terrorist 'assets' in Manchester and why the government did not warn the public of the threat in their midst – remain unanswered, deflected by the promise of an internal 'review'.

The alleged suicide bomber, Salman Abedi, was part of an extremist group, the Libyan Islamic Fighting Group, that thrived in Manchester and was cultivated and used by MI5 for more than 20 years.

The LIFG is proscribed by Britain as a terrorist organisation which seeks a 'hardline Islamic state' in Libya and 'is part of the wider global Islamist extremist movement, as inspired by Al-Qaeda'.

The 'smoking gun' is that when Theresa May was Home Secretary, LIFG jihadists were allowed to travel unhindered across Europe and encouraged to engage in 'battle': first to remove Mu'ammar Gaddafi in Libya, then to join Al-Qaeda affiliated groups in Syria.

Last year, the FBI reportedly placed Abedi on a 'terrorist watch list' and warned MI5 that his group was looking for a 'political target' in Britain. Why wasn't he apprehended and the network around him prevented from planning and executing the atrocity on 22 May?

These questions arise because of an FBI leak that demolished the 'lone wolf' spin in the wake of the 22 May attack – thus, the panicky, uncharacteristic outrage directed at Washington from London and Donald Trump's apology.

The Manchester atrocity lifts the rock of British foreign policy to reveal its Faustian alliance with extreme Islam, especially the sect known as Wahhabism or Salafism, whose principal custodian and banker is the oil kingdom of Saudi Arabia, Britain's biggest weapons customer.

This imperial marriage reaches back to the Second World War and the early days of the Muslim Brotherhood in Egypt. The aim of British policy was to stop pan-Arabism: Arab states developing a modern secularism, asserting their independence from the imperial West and controlling their resources. The creation of a rapacious Israel was meant to expedite this. Pan-Arabism has since been crushed; the goal now is division and conquest.

In 2011, according to Middle East Eye, the LIFG in Manchester were known as the 'Manchester boys'. Implacably opposed to Mu'ammar Gaddafi, they were considered high risk and a number were under Home Office control orders – house arrest – when anti-Gaddafi demonstrations broke out in Libya, a country forged from myriad tribal enmities.

Suddenly the control orders were lifted. 'I was allowed to go, no questions asked', said one LIFG member. MI5 returned their passports and counter-terrorism police at Heathrow airport were told to let them board their flights.

The overthrow of Gaddafi, who controlled Africa's largest oil reserves, had been long been planned in Washington and London. According to French intelligence, the LIFG made several assassination attempts on Gaddafi in the 1990s – bank-rolled by British intelligence. In March 2011, France, Britain and the US seized the opportunity of a 'humanitarian intervention' and attacked Libya. They were joined by NATO under cover of a UN resolution to 'protect civilians'.

Last September, a House of Commons Foreign Affairs Select Committee inquiry concluded that then Prime Minister David Cameron had taken the country to war against Gaddafi on a series of 'erroneous assumptions' and that the attack 'had led to the rise of Islamic State in North Africa'. The Commons committee quoted what it called Barack Obama's 'pithy' description of Cameron's role in Libya as a 'shit show'.

In fact, Obama was a leading actor in the 'shit show', urged on by his warmongering Secretary of State, Hillary Clinton, and a media accusing Gaddafi of planning 'genocide' against his own people. 'We knew... that if we waited one more day', said Obama, 'Benghazi, a city the size of Charlotte, could suffer a massacre that would have reverberated across the region and stained the conscience of the world.'

The massacre story was fabricated by Salafist militias facing defeat by Libyan government forces. They told Reuters there would be 'a real bloodbath, a massacre like we saw in Rwanda'. The Commons committee reported, 'The proposition that Mu'ammar Gaddafi would have ordered the massacre of civilians in Benghazi was not supported by the available evidence'.

Britain, France and the United States effectively destroyed Libya as a modern state. According to its own records, NATO launched 9,700 'strike sorties', of which more than a third hit civilian targets. They included fragmentation bombs and missiles with uranium warheads. The cities of Misurata and Sirte were carpet-bombed. Unicef, the UN children's organization, reported a high proportion of the children killed 'were under the age of ten'.

More than 'giving rise' to Islamic State — ISIS had already taken root in the ruins of Iraq following the Blair and Bush invasion in 2003 — these ultimate medievalists now had all of north Africa as a base. The attack also triggered a stampede of refugees fleeing to Europe.

Cameron was celebrated in Tripoli as a 'liberator', or imagined he was. The crowds cheering him included those secretly supplied and trained by Britain's SAS and inspired by Islamic State, such as the 'Manchester boys'.

To the Americans and British, Gaddafi's true crime was his iconoclastic independence and his plan to abandon the petrodollar, a pillar of American imperial power. He had audaciously planned to underwrite a common African currency backed by gold, establish an all-Africa bank and promote economic union among poor countries with prized resources. Whether or not this would have happened, the very notion was intolerable to the US as it prepared to 'enter' Africa and bribe African governments with military 'partnerships'.

The fallen dictator fled for his life. A Royal Air Force plane spotted his convoy, and in the rubble of Sirte, he was sodomized with a knife by a fanatic described in the news as 'a rebel'.

Having plundered Libya's $30 billion arsenal, the 'rebels' advanced south, terrorizing towns and villages. Crossing into sub-Saharan Mali, they destroyed that country's fragile stability. The ever-eager French sent planes and troops to their former colony 'to fight Al-Qaeda', or the menace they had helped create.

On 14 October 2011, President Obama announced he was sending special forces troops to Uganda to join the civil war there. In the next few months, US combat troops were sent to South Sudan, Congo and the Central African Republic. With Libya secured, an American invasion of the African continent was under way, largely unreported.

In London, one of the world's biggest arms fairs was staged by the British government. The buzz in the stands was the 'demonstration effect in Libya'. The London Chamber of Commerce and Industry held a preview entitled 'Middle East: A vast market for UK defence and security companies'. The host was the Royal Bank of Scotland, a major investor in cluster bombs, which were used extensively against civilian targets in Libya. The blurb for the bank's arms party lauded the 'unprecedented opportunities for UK defence and security companies'.

Last month, Prime Minister Theresa May was in Saudi Arabia, selling more of the £3 billion worth of British arms which the Saudis have used against Yemen. Based in control rooms in Riyadh, British military advisers assist the Saudi bombing raids, which have killed more than 10,000 civilians. There are now clear signs of famine. A Yemeni child dies every 10 minutes from preventable disease, says Unicef.

The Manchester atrocity on 22 May was the product of such unrelenting state violence in faraway places, much of it

British sponsored. The lives and names of the victims are almost never known to us.

This truth struggles to be heard, just as it struggled to be heard when the London Underground was bombed on 7 July 2005. Occasionally, a member of the public would break the silence, such as the east Londoner who walked in front of a CNN camera crew and reporter in mid-platitude. 'Iraq!' he said. 'We invaded Iraq. What did we expect? Go on, say it.'

At a large media gathering I attended, many of the important guests uttered 'Iraq' and 'Blair' as a kind of catharsis for that which they dared not say professionally and publicly.

Yet, before he invaded Iraq, Blair was warned by the Joint Intelligence Committee that 'the threat from Al-Qaeda will increase at the onset of any military action against Iraq... The worldwide threat from other Islamist terrorist groups and individuals will increase significantly.'

Just as Blair brought home to Britain the violence of his and George W Bush's blood-soaked 'shit show', so David Cameron, supported by Theresa May, compounded his crime in Libya and its horrific aftermath, including those killed and maimed in Manchester Arena on 22 May.

The spin is back, not surprisingly. Salman Abedi acted alone. He was a petty criminal, no more. The extensive network revealed last week by the American leak has vanished. But the questions have not.

Why was Abedi able to travel freely through Europe to Libya and back to Manchester only days before he committed his terrible crime? Was Theresa May told by MI5 that the FBI had tracked him as part of an Islamic cell planning to attack a 'political target' in Britain?

In the current election campaign, the Labour leader Jeremy

Corbyn has made a guarded reference to a 'war on terror that has failed'. As he knows, it was never a war on terror but a war of conquest and subjugation. Palestine. Afghanistan. Iraq. Libya. Syria. Iran is said to be next. Before there is another Manchester, who will have the courage to say that?

'Je ne sais pas qui je suis': Making Sense of Tragedies like the Charlie Hebdo Incident When the Government Narrative Doesn't Make Sense

Cynthia McKinney

January 2015

This paper seeks to establish that for citizens to turn their bellicose state into one that espouses peace, they must be aware of the operation not only of their Public State, but also of their Deep State. Moreover, this paper establishes that the Deep State acts for reasons that are not always readily apparent and in ways that are not always apparently legal. On some occasions, the Deep State even acts in ways that could be considered treasonous. The Public State then lies to cover up the actions of the Deep State. Insightful citizens understand government lies, but may not be aware of the operation of the Deep State. This paper argues that in order for citizens to turn belligerent governments into peaceful ones, they must understand that a powerful clue has been emitted whenever the government narrative doesn't make sense. Therefore, under these circumstances, the patriotic act is disbelief of the government narrative thereby rendering the actions of the Deep State dysfunctional. Finally, this paper examines the Charlie Hebdo tragedy in light of past 'Deep Events' that include the 1963 assassination of President John F. Kennedy and the 2005 London Bombing.

Charlie Hebdo Incident Details

According to a recent internet search, at least five major mainstream media outlets produced a timeline of the Charlie Hebdo events. On 7 January, the date of this murderous event, the Canadian Broadcasting Corporation (CBC) produced a timeline of events complete with a map and audio of an English-speaking witness.[1] The CBC article includes that the gunmen shouted 'Allahu Akbar' as they entered the Hebdo office. *The Telegraph* newspaper in London and *The International Business Times* in New York City followed suit on 8 January with their timelines.[2] *The Guardian, The Independent, EuroNews,* and CNN all published timelines, also. This is the most basic set of events in all of the timelines:

Just before 11:30 am car arrives in front of Charlie Hebdo office and two masked and hooded individuals get out. They are given access to the office by an employee just arriving for work.

Just after 11:30 am gunmen depart Hebdo office and engage in three police encounters that include gunfire and result in the death of one police officer lying on the ground. They carjack a car and make their getaway.

By 2:00 that afternoon, the hashtag (#) 'Je suis Charlie' had become a global social media trend.

Curiosities and Inconsistencies in the French Government Narrative Begin to Emerge

While Muslims all over the planet began to apologize for what had happened, citizen journalists and members of the global Truth Movement found inconsistencies in the details of the French Government's official narrative of the Charlie Hebdo events. At first, the video of the shooting of the police officer was blacked out. But later, un-blacked-out footage emerged that clearly showed that the police officer was not shot by the gunmen in the footage that had been circulated on most media websites. Even today, when we know that un-blacked-out footage exists and is widely available elsewhere, on *The International Business Times* website the blacked-out video is labelled with a caution: 'Graphic footage: Police officer shot by Paris gunmen'.[3]

Paul Craig Roberts, Ph.D., former Assistant Treasury Secretary for Economic Policy under Republican President Ronald Reagan, was among the first to publish his own compilation of inconvenient findings in his column, 'Suspicions are growing that the French shootings are a false flag operation'.[4] Roberts, noting that the effect of the tragic events was to bring France back into line after French President Hollande had spoken against Washington-inspired sanctions against Russia and to stop Europe's slide toward support of Palestinian aspirations for self-determination through a real and viable state, lists the following as questions, originally pointed out by members of the Truth Movement and unanswered by the official narrative:

a/ The suicide of the police chief in charge of the Hebdo investigation;
b/ YouTube's removal of the un-blacked-out video footage due to 'shocking and disgusting content';
c/ an analysis and display of the un-blacked-out video footage of the shooting of the police officer showing no blood, no recoil and no head fragments splattering.

On 13 January, Jonathan Cook, prize-winning journalist based in Nazareth, writing about the same un-blacked-out video as Roberts, that seems to show the police officer who the French government and media say was shot in the head, believes that he was in fact not shot in the head. After reviewing the video, Cook draws two conclusions: that the authorities lied about the cause of the policeman's death and the media simply 'regurgitated an official story that does not seem to fit the available evidence'.[5]

On 18 January 2015, the *Panamza* blog published an article that listed several inconsistencies. The article is entitled, 'Fuite des terrorists de Charlie Hebdo: un trajet impossible'.[6] This article describes the route of the Charlie Hebdo attackers as 'an impossible' one. This story is based on yet another video showing their departure as one that contradicts the official narrative. Finally, addressing this thorny issue, *Panamza* reports that Paris's Chief Prosecutor, François Molins, at a press conference on 9 January 2015, gives the getaway route of the perpetrators.

Sort of like the Warren Commission's Theory of the Magic Bullet that struck Texas Governor John Connolly and killed President Kennedy, but was substantially unscathed when found on a hospital stretcher.

Utilizing Google Maps, members of the public are seeking to answer the question, 'Which way did they go?'

Commenting further on yet another citizen analysis blog, the following commentary appears: 'I made an itinerary of the place where the first car was abandoned and the place where the attackers supposedly hijacked one of the witnesses. It is impossible. The witness lies.'

On 13 January 2015, Reuters published a video, republished by Panamza, that directly contradicted the official getaway version. In fact, the official getaway version caused more people familiar with the neighbourhood to join the Hebdo Truth Movement.

Finally, the revelation – not really, but just a reminder – of a chance encounter between French President Sarkozy and Amedy Coulibaly, where the latter asked the former for a job and then, years later, terrorized a Kosher grocery store![7]

Making Sense of the Nonsensical: The Rise of the Truth Movement

In my lifetime, the Truth Movement began the day everyone in the government subscribed to 'the Magic Bullet Theory' in the murder of President Kennedy. People who have impacted me deeply asked important questions at that time of a government that was not forthcoming. For example, in 2013, I had the opportunity to interview Dr Cyril Wecht, who investigated the President's autopsy report on behalf of the American Medical Association. He did not believe the official government narrative of what happened to President Kennedy after studying that report and did not believe it when I interviewed him 50 years later. Dr Cyril Wecht became a member of the Truth Movement only after he had been entrusted to study important information as a result of many objections to the government's narrative. Dr Wecht became a source of information and inspiration for many important others.

Inspection of the government's official narrative of the murder of Dr Martin Luther King, Jr also reveals certain anomalies that, at first, just don't add up. For example, it was testified in the 1999 trial establishing that there was a government conspiracy to murder Dr Martin Luther King, Jr, that the order was given by Jesse Jackson to have the local armed group, the Invaders, to leave the Lorraine Motel only minutes before the assassination. In order to make sense of all of the puzzle pieces individually and as a whole, each bit of information must be put into perspective by devising a completely new way of looking at it, even questioning 'conventional wisdom' – whatever that is.[8]

This questioning of conventional wisdom, or even what is taken to be the prevailing 'common sense' at the time, is what can produce breakthroughs in understanding. Like connecting the dots in that famous photograph of the black person touching Dr King on the balcony of the Lorraine Motel after he had been shot. According to testimony in the trial, that person was Merrell McCullough, then-officer with the Memphis Police Department, and infiltrator of the group the Invaders, later, at the time of the 1999 trial, employed by the Central Intelligence Agency (CIA).[9] Thus, yet another Truth Movement emerged around the murder of Dr King.

One of the popular street researchers in this area was Steve Cokely, who proclaimed at one of his lectures that his job was to translate the tedious minutiae of the 1999 trial into people-speak so that the average ordinary person who was impacted by the murder of Dr King could understand what had happened and why it mattered. Truth Warriors like Steve Cokely are never rewarded by the state – or for that matter, the public at large – and suffer like the whistleblowers that they are – for their dedication to getting the truth out about these tragic events. At best ignored by the special interest press, their daily labour is without recognition or award.

A powerful moment in the Truth Movement occurred when

JFK researchers joined with MLK researchers and then began delving into the facts of the other important assassinations of the decade: Malcolm X; President Kennedy's brother, Robert Kennedy, who himself was poised to become the next President of the United States. The COINTELPRO Papers provided a treasure trove of information on the government's orchestrated attacks on peace activists during the anti-Vietnam War era, as well as social movement activists working the streets of the US for social and economic justice for African-Americans, Puerto Ricans, American Indians, Mexican-Americans and their supporters.

The Church Committee went further and exposed assassination attempts on foreign leaders and the infiltration of every aspect of social, religious and academic life by US intelligence, including breaches of the US Constitution. What would be surprising is if a Truth Movement did not arise from the revelations.

After 9/11 2001, all members of Congress were told that we were hit because we were free and that we should tell that to our constituents. All over the US, members of Congress dutifully repeated that official narrative. But not me. I couldn't stoop so low when I understood that the United States had invested trillions of dollars in an intelligence and military infrastructure and on one day that infrastructure failed four times — including at the Pentagon itself! 9/11 created a new generation of Truthers because the US government's official narrative was so unbelievable. And as 9/11 is the excuse for draconian legislation that snatches civil liberties from US citizens and creates an illusion of support for US-led wars all over the world, more and more people are heeding Paul Craig Roberts's plea to people to just use their brains and think.

The Truth Movement as a Complex Adaptive System

A complex adaptive system (CAS) is a type of human organization and activity that produces new leadership and new knowledge. Complexity Leadership Theory seeks to explain new ways of acquiring knowledge in the 21st Century. Uhl-Bien calls it 'shifting leadership from the industrial age to the knowledge era'.[10]

According to Uhl-Bien, leadership models in the past were top-down, but now leadership is more organic, adaptive and emergent. According to Uhl-Bien, leadership today takes place in a more interactive and dynamic context: the Complex Adaptive System. Actors within the CAS have common goals and common needs. The individuals inside the CAS are linked in a kind of social system where they 'solve problems creatively and are able to learn and adapt quickly'.[11] I propose that the Truth Movement has become a complex adaptive system, brought into existence for the purpose of cutting through government lies on important and oftentimes tragic events.

This Truth CAS seeks to make sense of the nonsense that has been put forward by the Public State, and it produces new leaders who exercise a new kind of citizen leadership, not associated with position inside a bureaucracy or authority gained from a position. Thus, the members of the Truth CAS also represent something new: they are activated and empowered by the very fact of the Public State lies.

Members of a CAS adapt quickly to environmental conditions. They are interdependent and able to interact with each other and with the outside environment – in this case, the Public State. Members of a CAS also engage in a creative problem-solving process (trying to find the truth) which Uhl-

Bien defines as 'annealing'. This annealing is enhanced by interactions with a deceptive Public State that creates the need for more creativity and more problem-solving.

According to Uhl-Bien, 'the annealing process does however find solutions that individuals, regardless of their authority or expertise, could not find alone'.[12] According to Complexity Leadership Theory, this 'knowledge movement' is more capable of producing innovations and advances far more rapidly than what emerges 'from the isolated minds of individuals'.[13]

I suggest here that a Truth Movement that arises as a result of government lies is, in essence, a CAS that operates as a knowledge movement. I also posit here that not only are such movements inevitable, as all of the people are not willing to drop their critical analytical skills at the threshold of government propaganda, but that these movements represent the exercise of citizenship and patriotism due to their demand of truth in governance and the return to rule of law. In other words, 'you can fool some of the people all of the time and all of the people some of the time, but you can't fool all of the people all of the time'. And thus, a Truth Movement CAS is born.

'Je Ne Suis Pas Charlie; Je Suis Jean Charles de Menezes:' A London Execution Related to 7/7

After Jean Charles de Menezes was shot dead by three bullets to the head in a 2005 gross 'mistake', an emotional officer apologized to the victim's family, according to *The Telegraph*.[14] However, that error did not stop Scotland Yard from spying on the grieving family members, as was disclosed by *The Daily Mail* on 23 July 2014.[15]

According to Tom Cook, a Visiting Professor of Broadcast Journalism at Birmingham City University, 'Britain's rights to basic freedom of expression which writers, journalists, and free speech activists fought for over centuries have been sacrificed and abandoned in the space of a few short disastrous years'.[16] Cook chronicles police hacking of journalists' email, what he calls 'fearful self-censorship', and creeping powers of the state that exhibit signs of authoritarianism.

The Deep State Reveals Itself

Peter Dale Scott, Ph.D., theorized the Deep State when researching certain US events and popularized the concept in his eponymous book, *The American Deep State*. He noticed, when researching four Deep Events in US history – the assassination of President Kennedy, Watergate, Iran-Contra and 9/11 – that the events all bore certain common characteristics. In the US setting, these events all shared the fact of involvement of individuals who had access – either from the top or somewhere down the line – to the apparatus of the Continuity of Government (COG) for the United States. COG planning concerns itself with what happens in the US when/if a catastrophic event takes place.

Moreover, many of these events were carried out by the same individuals – whether they were in the government nominally or not! COG were the extreme measures that would be carried out even if they violated the Constitution because the Constitution would be suspended under this regime. Scott found that in the Iran-Contra scandal, the COG secret communications network was used to evade a Congressionally-mandated prohibition on the sale of weapons to Iran as well as financial support of the *Contras* who were, at that time, organized by the US to fight the Sandinista government of Nicaragua, headed by Daniel Ortega. Scott explains that, 'a very small group had access to a high-level secret network outside government review, in order to implement a program in opposition to government policy'.[17]

The COG planning was begun in the 1950s, but was continued and worked on by Dick Cheney and Donald Rumsfeld for two decades when, according to Scott, they implemented COG officially 'for the first time',[18] on 9/11 2001.

According to Scott's research, Iran-Contra and 9/11 were not the only Deep Events in which the US government's secret communication channel was utilized. In fact, this particular feature characterizes the environment in which the assassination of President Kennedy, Watergate, Iran-Contra and 9/11 took place. Therefore, Scott provides a powerful aspect of a Deep Event for the Truth Movement to research: the use of the government's secret communication channel. As a result, an important question for intrepid Charlie Hebdo Truthers is whether or not any French government secret communications channels were activated prior to or during the event.

Scott also identified three other characteristics of Deep Events that are worth bearing in mind as we digest the Charlie Hebdo tragedy: 1) a ready-made government explanation that is parroted by the press; 2) self-incriminating 'evidence' for the 'protected' individual(s) blamed by the government for causing or carrying out the tragedy; and 3) a small group of insider individuals able to control Deep Events and their aftermaths, including the narrative, the investigation and the cover-up.

Citizen journalists have been able to poke a considerable number of holes through the official French government narrative that has been expounded *ad nauseam* by the press. The fact that neither the government narrative nor the line of the parroting press changes in spite of new and contradictory evidence is alarming to these citizens who trust their skills of critical analysis more than they trust the utterances of their own governments. Therefore, it should not be surprising that more and more video evidence eventually becomes available, 'on the street' as it were, that does not conform to that official narrative.

In the case of 9/11, the government still refuses to release photographic and video evidence that might dispute its official narrative, leaving citizens to speculate about government intentions as well as about what else the government has lied. With as little as a cell phone, or the availability of the tools of social media – like Google Maps, for example – anyone can put their analytical skills to the test, record historic events or deconstruct government propaganda. All of this aids the task of citizen activists and alternative journalists. I have recounted just a few of those holes here.

True to form, the ID card left behind in the vehicle is as curious a piece of government evidence as was the passport that, in various official narratives, survived destruction despite the rubble of New York's evaporated World Trade Center buildings. This ID card bolsters the French government's explanation of who did what on that fateful January day, but it also conforms to Scott's prediction that Deep Events will provide self-incriminating evidence for the named patsy(ies). In the case of the murder of President Kennedy, it was Lee Harvey Oswald's own US intelligence activities that were intended to bolster his persona as a pro-Cuban Communist that came to be his undoing during his public unmasking as the government's guilty party.

From *Paris Match*, we have the story of one of the last men to have seen Hebdo cartoonists Cabu and Wolinsky alive. He is a market stand owner in one part of town, who sold newspapers to the cartoonists on the morning of their deaths but who also just happened to be the same person who was in the same and distant part of town as the Kouachi brothers after their deadly attack. This market stand owner was reportedly told by the Kouachi brothers, 'If the media ask you any questions, we are Al-Qaeda Yemen'.

A French citizen observer notes that while the much-celebrated identity card of Said Kouachi had been found in their hijacked getaway car, the driver's licence of Cherif Kouachi, Said's brother and accomplice, had also been left behind in the very same car! But even more than that, this very same witness, the market stand owner, was the owner of the car hijacked by the Kouachi brothers in which to make their getaway out of Paris. And, it was in this witness's car that the lost IDs were found!

Yet another French citizen observer asks how could the market stand owner travel from one part of Paris to another so quickly and have such fortuitous encounters with both the Hebdo cartoonists as well as their killers in the same day, all within a matter of minutes.[19] Where is there no traffic at all at 11.30 in the morning in a major US city? The Eleventh Arrondissement in Paris is the most densely populated in the city – almost twice that of Manhattan in New York City. How did the Kouachi brothers flee in the most densely populated neighbourhood in all of France?

Yet another 'witness' by the name of 'Eric', who lived next door to the Kouachi brothers, was interviewed by the press and was found to have known Wolinski 'very well' and Cabu 'somewhat'. This situation is similar to the 9/11 incident where an FBI informant actually lived with two of the alleged hijackers!

And then, we have the prior terror event in France involving an alleged terrorist (Merah) who happened to be an agent with France's now-disbanded anti-terrorism outfit.[20] The links between Al-Qaeda, the Islamic State (IS), also known as Daesh, and the United States government are inconvenient, well-known and not denied. They're just never mentioned in either the official narrative or that handed to us by the mainstream media. I label that media 'the special interest media' so that it becomes patently clear whose interest that media serves — not the public's or the people's. In fact, the special interest media are part and parcel of the Deep State, which could not operate its deceptions without media complicity. In fact, Jonathan Cook writes that 'one would expect "professional" journalism to respond by engaging with these concerns',[21] but instead, professional journalists meet these inconvenient facts with either silence or ridicule of the ones raising them.

Critical information, for example of David Headley's connection to US intelligence in the Mumbai blast is just never mentioned and left to swirl only in the realm of the 'coincidence evidence' that populates Truth Movements.[22] Or the inconvenient presence of war games or training exercises at the very moment of the 9/11 hijackings and the disappearance of the Malaysian Airlines plane MH370 over the Pacific Ocean and the London Tube bombing and the Boston Marathon Bombing.[23]

Mapping the route, questioning the accounts of the witnesses, studying video of the tragic events made public, remembering the magic passport and the connections to intelligence in previous recent terror tragedies, are all activities of a healthy state investigation and a healthy media. Unfortunately, this is exactly the kind of activity that has gone undone in public service quarters, yet thrives within a Truth Movement CAS. It is the annealing behaviour of Truth Movements flung across our globe that come together by way of social media and the internet, in the midst of the chaos of the moment, that helps us unmask and understand what is actually going on. These Truth Movements, then, are our last great hope to thwart the plans of the Deep State and reassert citizen rights to governance that respects rule of law and the human rights of all, including certain environmental rights of nature that nurtures and sustains us all.

Unmasking the Deep State is the best way to thwart its merger with the Public State — a circumstance that would render the political process and the operation of the Public State irrelevant to citizen values. If politics is the authoritative allocation of values in a society, then, in such a situation, the policies adopted by the Public State would bear no resemblance at all to the values of the citizens who elect it. Sadly, that is exactly the situation that many inside the US Truth Movement describe. And inside the peace movement, too. Activists inside these movements believe that halting the global slide towards what they believe is fascism is a matter of the political survival of the international rule of law and, in the US, of Constitutional governance.

I agree with them.

Therefore, there are hardly more important urgencies than

this. While not necessarily embracing one another's causes, it is imperative that disparate groups coalesce for this one single cause. The Deep State, operating under the official colour of the United States government, once wrote that misdirecting the public was one of its chief aims. This objective was announced in the FBI's COINTELPRO papers. The people's continued division is the Deep State's victory. So, too, of certain elements of the Truth Movement to not take these issues seriously.

Preventing the Merger of the Deep State and the Public State in Order to Make a Peace State

As a sitting Member of Congress, I was the first of 535 to demand an investigation of 9/11 and ask, 'What did the Bush Administration know and when did it know it'. That simple question, coming from me, was too much for our political system – or rather – for the Deep State to countenance.

Thanks to Dr Peter Dale Scott's important theoretical formulation, I can now make sense of the downward spiral that I was subjected to from all sides, including the hate message delivered over the public airwaves by a 'journalist' who, at the time, was on the FBI payroll. The Deep State won as I was put out of office and replaced by someone who would reliably vote for war while espousing 'peace' when necessary. The war machine rolls on, destroying individual lives and entire countries in its wake. My question, almost fourteen years later, has never been officially answered. Even while the events of 9/11 are used to justify every illegal US policy from the wars against Iraq, Afghanistan and Pakistan, Somalia and Yemen, to the wars at home against the Bill of Rights and the US Constitution. Yet it is only the Truth Movement that has come close in assessing what happened on that fateful day, and the global consequences of its aftermath.

Most of the current crop of Congress persons know from my example that the Deep State is riddled with landmines of self-protection. Best to say nothing, do nothing and know nothing — for any motion at all could set off a deadly device. And so, except for a few brave voices from unexpected places of power, officialdom is no closer to understanding what happened on 9/11 2001 and how it happened than on that sorrow-filled day. However, for true peace the world must know how 9/11 came to happen and then engulfed it in war.

Our goal is peace. At the same time, there are powerful individuals with access to state power who thwart our goal of peace. My personal formulation is that the bedrock for peace lies in truth. For without truth, there can be no justice. And without justice, there can be no peace. Going further, without peace there can be no dignity for us human beings or for the Earth that gives us life.

In 1963, President John F. Kennedy spoke at the graduation ceremony of American University. And in that speech, President Kennedy used the word 'peace' over thirty times in a speech lasting less than thirty minutes. President Eisenhower, before Kennedy was sworn in as President, warned the people of the United States against the machinations of the Military–Industrial Complex. Today, that Complex has also absorbed Wall Street, which in turn has swallowed Congress and the media.

Instead of turning back the Deep State, the people of the US have allowed the Deep State to encroach further and further into the public sphere. Some of this is caused by the collaboration of activists inside the Truth Movement, knowingly or unknowingly, with the mechanisms of the Deep State. Yet far more pervasive is the fact of public lack of awareness of this aspect of governance. With access to illicit proceeds from drug trafficking and other illegal activities, the Deep State of the US has almost unlimited funds with which to co-opt and corrupt officials in the Public State all over the world.

Jonathan Cook concludes: 'We have to trust that the officials haven't lied to the journalists and that the journalists haven't misled us. And yet there are no grounds for that trust apart from blind faith that our officials are honest and not self-interested, and that our journalists are competent and independent-minded.'[24] I agree with him. And part of the importance of Scott's research is how he demonstrates that a very small group of insiders can implement a programme 'in opposition to government policy'. I do believe that the other side of that coin is also operative: that is, that a very small group of courageous insiders or individuals, like the activists who broke into the FBI office in order to expose the excesses of COINTELPRO, can make a huge difference in saving our government from its current cabal of controllers.

I encourage the Truth Movements around the world to continue their brave questioning of official narratives that seem ready-made in the face of tragedies. While I have nothing to offer them except the knowledge that there is life after whistleblowing, whistleblowers, even while suffering greatly under the administration of President Barack Obama, must continue to act on their consciences and we must support them in every way that we can. For today, we are on the path of a fusion between the Deep State and the Public State.

If we are successful, we will be able, finally, to stop the wars and the immobilizing madness of hatred and division and place the US squarely on the path of truth, reconciliation and peace. If the Deep State is able to beat back our Truth and Knowledge movements, I shudder to even contemplate what our future holds.

Notes

1. CBC News, 'Charlie Hebdo newspaper shooting timeline: At least a dozen are dead, and numerous people were injured', 7 January 2015 located at http://www.cbc.ca/news/world/charlie-hebdo-newspaper-shooting-timeline-1.2892399 accessed on 30 January 2015.
2. *Telegraph* and *International Business Times* timelines are located at http://www.telegraph.co.uk/news/worldnews/europe/france/11332548/Charlie-Hebdo-timeline-from-defiance-to-tragedy-and-mourning.html and http://www.ibtimes.com/paris-attack-video-gunmen-filmed-shooting-wounded-police-officer-1776004 respectively, accessed on 30 January 2015.
3. Shuan Sim, 'Paris Attack Video: Gunmen Filmed Shootout with Police Officer', *International Business Times*, http://www.ibtimes.com/paris-attack-video-gunmen-filmed-shooting-wounded-police-officer-1776004.
4. Paul Craig Roberts, 'Suspicions are growing that the French shootings are a false flag operation', located at http://www.paulcraigroberts.org/2015/01/11/suspicions-growing-french-shootings-false-flag-operation/ accessed on 30 January 2015.
5. Jonathan Cook, 'What Hebdo execution video really shows', 13 January 2015 located at http://www.jonathan-cook.net/blog/2015-01-13/what-hebdo-execution-video-really-shows/ accessed on 30 January 2015.
6. Panamza, 'Fuite des terrorists de Charlie Hebdo: un trajet impossible', located at http://www.panamza.com/180115-charlie-trajet accessed on 29 January 2015.
7. *Le Parisien*, 'Amedi, 27 ans, rencontre Sarkozy cet après-midi', 15 July 2009 located at http://www.leparisien.fr/grigny-91350/amedi-27-ans-

rencontre-sarkozy-cet-apres-midi-15-07-2009-580211.php#xtref=
http%3A%2F%2Fwww.google.fr%2Furl%3Fsa%3Dt%24rct%3Dj
%24q%3D%24esrc%3Ds%24source%3Dweb%24cd%3D9%24ved
%3D0CE8QFjAI%24url%3Dhttp%253A%252F
%252Fwww.leparisien.fr%252Fgrigny-91350%252Famedi-27-ans-
rencontre-sarkozy-cet-apres-midi-15-07-2009-580211.php%24ei
%3DOfivVLSMNYbkaLWVgKgG%24usg%3DAFQjCNHtjA22qn1xi
TvoTE16EKrVwN_TXQ%24sig2%3Dc9KGt77MhRW-
gUoWjXnNhg%24bvm%3Dbv.83339334%2Cd.d2s accessed on 30 January 2015.

8. *Complete Transcript of the Martin Luther King, Jr. Assassination Conspiracy Trial*, Testimony of Charles Cabbage, 161 – 162 located at http://www.thekingcenter.org/sites/default/files/Assassination%20Trial%20-%20Full%20Transcript.pdf accessed on 30 January 2015.

9. *Complete Trial Transcript*, Testimony of Dr Smith, 141 located at http://www.thekingcenter.org/sites/default/files/Assassination%20Trial%20-%20Full%20Transcript.pdf accessed on 30 January 2015.

10. Mary Uhl-Bien, Russ Marion, Bill McKelvey, 'Complexity Leadership Theory: Shifting leadership from the industrial age to the knowledge era', *The Leadership Quarterly*, 18 (2007): 298–318.

11. Uhl-Bien, Marion, and McKelvey, 'Complexity Leadership Theory', 299.

12. Ibid., 303.

13. Ibid.

14. Nick Allen, 'Police marksman who shot Jean Charles de Menezes apologises to family', 24 October 2008, located at http://www.telegraph.co.uk/news/uknews/law-and-order/3254455/Police-marksman-who-shot-Jean-Charles-de-Menezes-apologises-to-family.html accessed on 30 January 2015.

15. Stephen Wright, 'Undercover police 'spied on the de menezes [sic] family': Secret probe after Brazilian shot dead in catastrophic blunder', *The Daily Mail*, 23 July 2014 located at http://www.dailymail.co.uk/news/article-2703451/Undercover-police-spied-Menezes-family-

Secret-probe-Brazilian-shot-dead-catastrophic-blunder.html accessed on 30 January 2015.
16. Tom Cook, 'Press freedom in Britain has been "sacrificed"', January 29, 2015 located at http://nsnbc.me/2015/01/29/press-freedom-in-britain-has-been-sacrificed/ accessed on 29 January 2015.
17. Peter Dale Scott, Ph.D., 'The Hidden Government Group Linking JFK, Watergate, Iran–Contra, and 9/11', 5 October 2014 located at http://whowhatwhy.com/2014/10/05/the-hidden-government-group-linking-jfk-watergate-iran-contra-and-911/#sthash.pYX3miMH.dpuf accessed on 28 January 2014.
18. Ibid.
19. Google Maps provides a breakdown of the official narrative route archived by one citizen observer located at https://www.google.fr/maps/dir/48.8807004,2.3728185/48.8784144,2.374224/@48.8789788,2.3730116,17z accessed on 30 January 2015.
20. LePoint.fr, 'Mohamed Merah travaillait pour les RG: La DCRI est chargée de L'enquete sur les meurtres commis par le djihadiste. Allors qu'elle est elle-meme mise en cause', 7 June 2012 located at http://www.lepoint.fr/societe/merah-une-enquete-a-haut-risque-07-06-2012-1470689_23.php accessed on 30 January 2015.
21. Jonathan Cook, 'Hebdo video', located at http://www.jonathan-cook.net/blog/2015-01-13/what-hebdo-execution-video-really-shows/ accessed on 30 January 2015.
22. See Dean Nelson, 'Mumbai suspect is US double agent, India claims', 16 December 2009 located at http://www.telegraph.co.uk/news/worldnews/northamerica/usa/6826571/Mumbai-suspect-is-US-double-agent-India-claims.html accessed on 30 January 2015.
23. For more information on 9/11 war games see http://www.911myths.com/index.php/War_Games and for information on the war games training taking place just before and after the Malaysian airliner went missing see http://www.smh.com.au/entertainment/books/first-book-on-mh370-mystery-blames-us-war-games-20140517-38gmf.html; for information on exercises taking place at the time of the 7/7 London bombing see https://www.youtube.com/watch?v=E1HPNpxbfX8; and for informa-

tion on the police exercises that were taking place on the day of the Boston Marathon Bombing see http://www.dailymotion.com/video/xz3pz1_boston-marathon-bombing-the-fbi-and-bomb-drills-ben-swann-on-reality-check_news all accessed on 30 January 2015.
24. Jonathan Cook, 'Hebdo video', located at http://www.jonathan-cook.net/blog/2015-01-13/what-hebdo-execution-video-really-shows/ accessed on 30 January 2015.

About the Contributors

NOAM CHOMSKY
Dr Chomsky is Professor Emeritus at the Massachusetts Institute of Technology. He received his PhD from the University of Pennsylvania for his work on linguistics after which he was appointed to the Harvard Society of Fellows. The Vietnam War compelled Dr Chomsky to dedicate more time to activism. Since then, he has travelled the world lecturing and writing. His many books include *On Western Terrorism* (with Andre Vltchek), *On Palestine* (with Ilan Pappé), *Who Rules the World?* and *Requiem for the American Dream* (with Peter Hutchison, Kelly Nyks and Jared P. Scott).

T.J. COLES
Coles received his PhD from Plymouth University (UK) in 2017 for work on the aesthetic experiences of blind and visually impaired people, which draws on the philosophy of cognitive psychology and neuroscience. He is also a columnist with Axis of Logic and the author of *Britain's Secret Wars*, *The Great Brexit Swindle*, and *President Trump, Inc.* (all Clairview Books).

BRUCE K. GAGNON
Bruce is coordinator and co-founder of the Global Network Against Weapons and Nuclear Energy in Space, an active member of Veterans for Peace and Secretary of Space in the Green Shadow Cabinet. Having organized numerous large-scale protests against Trident II, Cassini, and other dangerous

ABOUT THE CONTRIBUTORS | 127

initiatives, he has travelled the world giving talks to peace groups and universities. His articles have appeared in numerous magazines and journals. Bruce is the author of *Come Together Right Now* and hosts *The Issue*.

KATHY KELLY

A war-tax refuser since 1980, Kathy has travelled the world as a peace and solidarity activist, visiting Bosnia, Haiti and Iraq. She is the Coordinator of Voices for Creative Non-Violence, a regular writer for teleSUR and co-founder of Voices in the Wilderness — a campaign to end the genocidal sanctions inflicted by Britain and America upon Iraq (1990–2003). Kathy has made fifteen trips to Afghanistan and, as an invited guest of the Afghan Peace Volunteers, has lived alongside ordinary Afghans in a working-class area of Kabul.

CYNTHIA MCKINNEY

Dr McKinney served her home state of Georgia in its legislature for four years and the United States for twelve years in Congress, receiving her PhD in Leadership and Change at Antioch University. Dr McKinney has travelled to war-torn Gaza and Libya as an aid worker and observer. She has spoken at the European Parliament in a conference attended by members of the Philippine Independence Movement and international leaders of Kurdish and Tamil human rights groups. A juror on the Bertrand Russell Tribunal for Palestine, Cynthia has also been involved with the Perdana Global Peace Foundation, the Brussells Tribunal on Iraq and a successful effort in Spain to indict members of the Rwandan Patriotic Army who committed genocide in the Democratic Republic of Congo.

ILAN PAPPÉ

Dr Pappé is Professor of History at the University of Exeter and Director of the European Centre for Palestine Studies. He founded and directed the Academic Institute for Peace in Givat Haviva, Israel, between 1992 and 2000 and was the Chair of the Emil Tuma Institute for Palestine Studies in Haifa between 2000 and 2006. Professor Pappé was a senior lecturer in the department of Middle Eastern History and the Department of Political Science in Haifa University, Israel, between 1984 and 2006. He is the author of numerous books, including *The Ethnic Cleansing of Palestine*, *The Idea of Israel*, and *On Palestine* (with Noam Chomsky).

JOHN PILGER

John is the recipient of numerous honorary doctorates and titles, including the Edward Wilson Fellowship from Deakin University, Melbourne, Frank H.T. Rhodes Professorship from Cornell University, and Oxford Brookes University. A prolific filmmaker, he has made sixty documentaries to date, all of which challenge establishment claims, from healthcare to nuclear weapons. A regular writer for popular magazines and newspapers, John has won over twenty major awards, including an Emmy, the UN Media Peace Prize, a BAFTA, the Reporters Sans Frontières Award and many others. In 2003 he was awarded the prestigious Sophie Prize for '30 years of exposing injustice and promoting human rights'. In 2009, he was awarded the Sydney Peace Prize.

ROBIN RAMSAY

Robin is a writer and editor. He has authored a number of books and pamphlets, several of which are still available. For ten years he wrote a column for the *Fortean Times* on conspiracy theories. In 1983 he co-founded *Lobster* magazine, which is still going (www.lobster.magazine.co.uk) and is currently his central focus.

BRIAN TERRELL

A writer, researcher and activist, Brian volunteers for Voices for Creative Non-Violence, which he co-coordinates. He lives a philosophy of self-sufficiency, residing and working at Strangers and Guests Farm in Maloy, Iowa. He and his partner raise most of what they need from their gardens, chickens and goats. Brian travels, speaks and acts with various communities working for peace. In February 2015 he returned from his second visit to Kabul, Afghanistan.

Books to challenge   your perception of reality

A message from Clairview

We are an independent publishing company with a focus on cutting-edge, non-fiction books. Our innovative list covers current affairs and politics, health, the arts, history, science and spirituality. But regardless of subject, our books have a common link: they all question conventional thinking, dogmas and received wisdom.

Despite being a small company, our list features some big names, such as Booker Prize winner Ben Okri, literary giant Gore Vidal, world leader Mikhail Gorbachev, modern artist Joseph Beuys and natural childbirth pioneer Michel Odent.

So, check out our full catalogue online at
www.clairviewbooks.com
and join our emailing list for news on new titles.

office@clairviewbooks.com

CLAIRVIEW